MOBILIZING WOMAN-POWER

BY

HARRIOT STANTON BLATCH

British Library Cataloguing-in-Publication Data
A catalogue record for this book is available from the
British Library

CONTENTS

MOBILIZING WOMAN-POWER

ILLUSTRATIONS

Introduction to the

World War One Centenary Series

The First World War was a global war centred in Europe that began on 28 July 1914 and lasted until 11 November 1918. More than nine million combatants were killed, a casualty rate exacerbated by the belligerents' technological and industrial sophistication – and tactical stalemate. It was one of the deadliest conflicts in history, paving the way for major political changes, including revolutions in many of the nations involved. The war drew in all the world's great economic powers, which were assembled in two opposing alliances: the Allies (based on the Triple Entente of the United Kingdom, France and the Russian Empire) and the Central Powers of Germany and Austria-Hungary. These alliances were both reorganised and expanded as more nations entered the war: Italy, Japan and the United States joined the Allies, and the Ottoman Empire and Bulgaria joined the Central Powers. Ultimately, more than 70 million military personnel were mobilised.

The war was triggered by the assassination of Archduke Franz Ferdinand of Austria, heir to the throne of Austria-Hungary, by a Yugoslav nationalist, Gavrilo Princip in Sarajevo, June 28th 1914. This set off a diplomatic crisis when Austria-Hungary delivered an ultimatum to Serbia, and international alliances were invoked. Within weeks, the major powers were at war and the conflict soon spread around the world. By the end of the war, four major imperial powers; the German, Russian, Austro-Hungarian and Ottoman empires— ceased to exist. The map of Europe was redrawn, with several independent nations restored or created. On peace, the League of Nations formed with the aim of preventing any repetition of such an appalling conflict, encouraging cooperation and communication between the newly autonomous nation states. This laudatory pursuit failed spectacularly with the advent of the Second World War however, with new European nationalism and the rise of fascism paving the way for the next global crisis.

This book is part of the World War One Centenary series; creating, collating and reprinting new and old works of poetry, fiction, autobiography and analysis. The series forms a commemorative tribute to mark the passing of one of the world's bloodiest wars, offering new perspectives on this tragic yet fascinating period of human history.

Amelia Carruthers

A Timeline of the Major Events of World War One in Europe

1914

28th June	Franz Ferdinand Assassinated at Sarajevo.
29th June	Austro-Hungary send despatch to Vienna accusing Serbian complicity in the killing.
5th July	Kaiser Wilhelm promises German support for Austria against Serbia.
20th July	Austria-Hungary sends troops to the Serbian frontier.
25th July	Serbia mobilises its troops, Russia sends troops to the Austrian frontier.
28th July	Austria-Hungary Declares war on Serbia.

29th July	Austrians bombard Belgrade and German patrols cross the French border. Britain warns it cannot remain neutral.
1st August	Germany declares war on Russia. Italy and Belgium announce neutrality. French mobilisation ordered.
3rd August	Germany declares war on France and invades Belgium (Schlieffen plan). Great Britain mobilises.
4th August	Britain declares war on Germany and Austria-Hungary (after ultimatum to stand down). US declares neutrality. Germany declares war on Belgium.
6th August	First British casualties with the HMS Amphion sunk by German mines in the North sea. 150 men dead.
7th August	First members of the BEF (British Expeditionary Force) arrive in France.

11th August	Start of enlisting for Kitchener's New Army 'Your King and Country Need You'.
20th August	Brussels is evacuated as German troops occupy the city.
23rd August	The BEF started its retreat from Mons. Germany invades France.
26th August	Russian army defeated at Tannenburg and Masurian Lakes. BEF suffers over 7000 casualties at the Battle of Le Cateau –forced to retreat.
6th September	Battle of the Marne starts; checks German advance, but at the cost of 13,000 British, 250,000 French and 250,000 German casualties.
19th October	First Battle of Ypres.
29th October	Turkey enters the war (on Germany's side).
22nd November	Trenches are now established along the entire Western Front.
8th December	Battle of the Falkland Islands.

1915

| 19th January | First Zeppelin raid on Britain (Great Yarmouth and Kings Lynn – killing 5). |

19th January | First Zeppelin raid on Britain (Great Yarmouth and Kings Lynn – killing 5).

18th February | Blockade of Great Britain by German U-boats begins. All vessels considered viable targets, including neutrals.

22nd April | Second Battle of Ypres begins. Widespread use of poison gas by Germany.

25th April | Allied troops land in Gallipoli.

2nd May | Austro-German offensive on Galicia begins.

7th May | The Lusitania is sunk by a German U-Boat – creating US/German diplomatic crisis.

23rd May | Italy declares war on Germany and Austria

31st May | First Zeppelin raid on London, killing 35 and shaking morale.

30th June	German troops use flamethrowers for the first time, against the British at Hooge, Ypres.
5th August	Germany captures Warsaw from the Russians.
21st August	Final British offensive in the Dardanelles (Scimitar Hill, Gallipoli). They lose, and suffer 5000 deaths.
25th September	Start of the Battle of Loos and Champagne. The British use gas for the first time, but the wind blows it over their own troops, resulting in 2632 casualties.
31st October	Steel helmets introduced on the British Front.
15th December	Sir Douglas Haig replaces Sir John French as Commander of the BEF.

1916

8th January	Allied evacuation of Helles marks the end of the Gallipoli campaign.
21st February	Start of the Battle of Verdun – German offensive against the Mort-Homme Ridge. The battle lasts 10 months and over a million men become casualties. (Finishes 18th December, the longest and costliest battle of the Western Front).
9th March	Germany declares war on Portugal. Six days later, Austria follows suit.
31st May	Battle of Jutland – lasts until 1st June. German High Seas Fleet is forced to retire despite having inflicted heavier losses on the Royal Navy (14 ships and 6,100 men). German fleet irreparably damaged.
4th June	Start of the Russian Brusilov Offensive on the Eastern front. Nearly cripples Austro-Hungary.

1st July	Start of the Battle of the Somme – 750,000 allied soldiers along a 25 mile front. Nearly 60,000 are dead or wounded on the first day.
14th July	Battle of Bazetin Ridge marks the end of the first Somme Offensive. The British break the German line but fail to deploy cavalry fast enough to take advantage. 9,000 men are lost.
23rd July	Battle of Pozières Ridge marks the second Somme Offensive, costs 17,000 allied casualties – the majority of whom are Australian. (ends 7th August).
10th August	End of the Brusilov Offensive.
9th September	The Battle of Ginchy. The British capture Ginchy – a post of vital strategic importance as it commands a view of the whole battlefield.
15th September	First use en masse of tanks at the Somme. The Battle of Flers-Courcelette signifies the start of the third stage of the Somme offensive.

13th November	Battle of Ancre. The fourth phase of the Somme Offensive is marked by the British capturing Beaumont Hamel and St. Pierre Division, taking nearly 4,000 prisoners.
12th December	Germany delivers Peace Note to Allies suggesting compromise.

1917

1st February   Germany's unrestricted submarine warfare campaign starts.

3rd February   US sever diplomatic relations with Germany as U-boats threaten US shipping. Intercepted messages reveal that Germany is provoking the Mexicans into war with the US.

21st February   The great German withdrawal begins. Serre, Miraumont, Petit Miraumont, Pys and Warlencourt are evacuated, falling back 25 miles to establish stronger positions on the Hindenburg Line.

15th March   Tsar Nicholas II abdicates as Moscow falls to Russian Revolutionaries. Demise of the Russian army frees German troops for the Western front.

6th April   USA declares war on Germany – troops mobilise immediately.

9th April	Battle of Arras. British successfully employ new tactics of creeping barrages, the 'graze fuse' and counter battery fire.
16th April	France launches an unsuccessful offensive on the Western Front. – Second Battle of Aisne begins as part of the 'Nivelle Offensive'. Losses are horrendous, triggering mutinies in the French Army.
7th June	The Battle of Messines Ridge. British succeed with few casualties, detonating 19 mines under German front lines – the explosions are reportedly heard from England.
13th June	Germans launch first major heavy bomber raid of London – kills and injures 594.
25th June	First US troops arrive in France.
31st July	Start of the Third Battle at Ypres – a 15 mile front in Flanders. Initial attacks are successful as the German forward trenches are lightly manned.

15th August	The Battle of Lens (Hill 70). – Canadians at the forefront , won a high vantage point, though loss of 9,200 men.
20th August	Third Battle of Verdun begins. French progress is marked by gaining lost territory in the earlier battles.
9th October	The third phase of the Ypres Offensive begins with British and French troops taking Poelcapelle. 25mm of rain falls in 48 hours and the battlefield turns into a quagmire.
12th October	British launch assault at Ypres Against the Passchendale Ridge. New Zealand and Australians take terrible casualties. Bogged down in mud and forced back to start lines.
24th October	Battle of Caporetto – Italian Army heavily defeated.
26th October	Second Battle of Passchendaele begins, 12,000 men lost and 300 yards gained (ends 10th November – 500,000 casualties,

140,000 deaths and 5 miles gained).

6th November	Britain launches major offensive on the Western Front.

6th November

Britain launches major offensive on the Western Front.

20th November

Victory for British tanks at Cambrai - The Royal flying Corps drop bombs at the same time on German anti-tank guns and strong points. Early example of the 'Blitzkrieg' tactics later used by Germany in World War Two.

5th December

Armistice between Germany and Russia signed.

1918

16th January

Riots in Vienna and Budapest with dissatisfaction at the war.

3rd March

Treaty of Brest-Litovsk signed between (Soviet) Russia and Germany.

21st March

Second Battle of the Somme marked by the German spring offensive, the 'Kaiserschlacht'. Germans attack along a 50 mile front south of Arras.

22nd March

Victory for Germany with operation Michael - Use of new 'Storm trooper' assault to smash through British positions west of St. Quentin, taking 16,000 prisoners.

23rd March

Greatest air battle of the war takes place over the Somme, with 70 aircraft involved.

5th April

The German Spring Offensive halts outside Amiens as British and Australian forces hold the Line. The second 1917 battle of the Somme ends, as Germany calls off operation Michael.

9th April	Germany starts offensive in Flanders –Battle of the Lys (ends 29th April).
19th May	German air force launches largest raid on London, using 33 aircraft.
27th May	Operation Blucher – The Third German Spring Offensive attacks the French army along the Aisne River. French are forced back to the Marne, but hold the river with help from the Americans.
15th July	Second battle of the Marne started; final phase of German spring offensive. Start of the collapse of the German army with irreplaceable casualties.
8th August	Second Battle of Amiens – German resistance sporadic and thousands surrender.
27th September	British offensive on the Cambrai Front leads to the storming of the Hindenburg Line. Battle of St.

	Quentin – British and U.S troops launch devastating offensives.
4th October	Germany asks the allies for an armistice (sent to Woodrow Wilson).
8th October	Allies advance along a 20 mile front from St. Quentin to Cambrai, driving the Germans back and capturing 10,000 troops.
29th October	Germany's navy mutinies (at Jade).
3rd November	Austria makes peace. German sailors mutiny at Kiel.
9th November	Kaiser Wilhelm abdicates and revolution breaks out in Berlin.
11th November	Germany signs the armistice with the allies – coming into effect at 11.00am (official end of WWI).

1919

10th January	Communist Revolt in Berlin (Battle of Berlin).
18th January	Paris Peace Conference Begins.
25th January	Principle of a League of Nations ratified.
6th May	Under conditions of the Peace conference, German colonies are annexed.
21st June	The surrendered German naval fleet at Scapa Flow was scuttled.
28th June	Treaty of Versailles signed.
19th July	Cenotaph unveiled in London.

By Amelia Carruthers

Munition Wages

Earning high wages?
Yus, Five quid a week.
A woman, too, mind you,
I calls it dim sweet.

Ye'are asking some questions –
But bless yer, here goes:
I spends the whole racket
On good times and clothes.

Me saving? Elijah!
Yer do think I'm mad.
I'm acting the lady,
But – I ain't living bad.

I'm having life's good times.
See 'ere, it's like this:
The 'oof come o' danger,
A touch-and-go bizz.

We're all here today, mate,
Tomorrow – perhaps dead,
If Fate tumbles on us
And blows up our shed.

Afraid! Are yer kidding?
With money to spend!
Years back I wore tatters,

Now – silk stockings, mi friend!

I've bracelets and jewellery,
Rings envied by friends;
A sergeant to swank with,
And something to lend.

I drive out in taxis,
Do theatres in style.
And this is mi verdict –
It is jolly worth while.

Worth while, for tomorrow
If I'm blown to the sky,
I'll have repaid mi wages
In death – and pass by.

By Madeline Ida Bedford 'Munition Wages'

Image 1. US Kanning Kitchen

"The home front is always underrated by Generals in the field. And yet that is where the Great War was won and lost. The Russian, Bulgarian, Austrian and German home fronts fell to pieces before their armies collapsed."

British Prime Minister Lloyd George, in his 'War Memoirs'

MOBILIZING WOMAN-POWER

TO THE ABLE AND DEVOTED WOMEN OF GREAT BRITAIN AND FRANCE

Who have stood behind the armies of the Allies through the years of the Great War as an unswerving second line of defense against an onslaught upon the liberty and civilization of the world, I dedicate this volume.

HARRIOT STANTON BLATCH

Jeanne d'Arc.--the spirit of the women of
the Allies.

FOREWORD

It is a real pleasure to write this foreword to the book which Mrs. Harriot Stanton Blatch dedicates to the women of Great Britain and France; to the women who through the years of the great war have stood as the second line of defense against the German horror which menaces the liberty and civilization of the entire world.

There could be no more timely book. Mrs. Blatch's aim is to stir the women of this country to the knowledge that this is their war, and also to make all our people feel that we, and especially our government, should welcome the service of women, and make use of it to the utmost. In other words, the appeal of Mrs. Blatch is essentially an appeal for service. No one has more vividly realized that service benefits the one who serves precisely as it benefits the one who is served. I join with her in the appeal that the women shall back the men with service, and that the men in their turn shall frankly and eagerly welcome the rendering of such service *on the basis of service by equals for a common end.*

Mrs. Blatch makes her appeal primarily because of the war needs of the moment. But she has in view no less the great tasks of the future. I welcome her book as an answer to the cry that the admission of women to an equal share in the right of self government will tend to soften the body politic. Most certainly I will ever set my face like flint against any unhealthy softening of our civilization, and as an answer in advance to hypercriticism I explain that I do not mean softness in the sense of tender-heartedness; I mean the softness which, extends to the head and to the moral fibre, I mean the softness which manifests itself either in unhealthy sentimentality or in a materialism which may be either thoughtless and pleasure-loving or sordid and money-getting. I believe that the best women, when thoroughly aroused, and when the right appeal is made to them, will offer our surest means of resisting this unhealthy softening.

No man who is not blind can fail to see that we have entered a new day in the great epic march of the ages. For good or for evil the old days have passed; and it rests with us, the men and women now alive, to decide whether in the new days the world is to be a better or a worse place to live in, for our descendants.

In this new world women are to stand on an equal footing with men, in ways and to an extent never hitherto dreamed of. In this country they are on the eve of securing, and in much of the country have already secured, their full political rights. It is imperative that they should understand, exactly as it is imperative that men should understand, that such rights are of worse than no avail, unless the will for the performance of duty goes hand in hand with the acquirement of the privilege.

If the women in this country reinforce the elements that tend to a softening of the moral fibre, to a weakening of the will, and unwillingness to look ahead or to face hardship and labor and danger for a high ideal--then all of us alike, men and women, will suffer. But if they show, under the new conditions, the will to develop strength, and the high idealism and the iron resolution which under less favorable circumstances were shown by the women of the Revolution and of the Civil War, then our nation has before it a career of greatness never hitherto equaled. This book is fundamentally an appeal, not that woman shall enjoy any privilege unearned, but that hers shall be the right to do more than she has ever yet done, and to do it on terms of self-respecting partnership with men. Equality of right does not mean identity of function; but it does necessarily imply identity of purpose in the performance of duty.

Mrs. Blatch shows why every woman who inherits the womanly virtues of the past, and who has grasped the ideal of the added womanly virtues of the present and the future, should support this war with all her strength and soul. She testifies from personal knowledge to the hideous brutalities shown toward women and children by the Germany of to-day; and she adds the fine sentence: "Women fight for a place in the sun for those who hold right above might."

She shows why women must unstintedly give their labor in order to win this war; and why the labor of the women must be used to back up both the labor and the fighting work of the men, for the fighting men leave gaps in the labor world which must be filled by the work of women. She says in another sentence worth remembering, "The man behind the counter should of course be moved to a muscular employment; but we must not interpret his dalliance with tapes and ribbons as a proof of a superfluity of men."

Particularly valuable is her description of the mobilization of women in Great Britain and France. From these facts she draws the conclusion as to America's needs along this very line. She paints as vividly as I have ever known painted, the truth as to why it is a merit that women should be forced to work, a merit that *every one* should be forced to work! It is just as good for women as for men that they should have to use body and mind, that they should not be idlers. As she puts it, "Active mothers insure a virile race. The peaceful nation, if its women fall victims to the luxury which rapidly increasing wealth brings, will decay." "Man power must give itself unreservedly at the front. Woman power must show not only eagerness but fitness to substitute for man power."

I commend especially the chapter containing the sentence, "This war may prove to us the wisdom and economy of devoting public funds to mothers rather than to crèches and juvenile asylums;" and also the chapter in which the author tells women that if they are merely looking for a soft place in life their collective demand for a fair field and no favor will be wholly ineffective. The doors for service now stand open, and it rests with the women themselves to say whether they will enter in!

The last chapter is itself an unconscious justification of woman's right to a share in the great governmental decisions which to-day are vital. No statesman or publicist could set forth more clearly than Mrs. Blatch the need of winning this war, in order to prevent either endless and ruinous wars in the future, or else a world despotism which would mean the atrophy of everything that really tends to the elevation of mankind.

Mrs. Blatch has herself rendered a very real service by this appeal that women should serve, and that men should let them serve.

Theodore Roosevelt

I
OUR FOE

The nations in which women have influenced national aims face the nation that glorifies brute force. America opposes the exaltation of the glittering sword; opposes the determination of one nation to dominate the world; opposes the claim that the head of one ruling family is the direct and only representative of the Creator; and, above all, America opposes the idea that might makes right.

Let us admit the full weight of the paradox that a people in the name of peace turns to force of arms. The tragedy for us lay in there being no choice of ways, since pacific groups had failed to create machinery to adjust vital international differences, and since the Allies each in turn, we the last, had been struck by a foe determined to settle disagreements by force.

Never did a nation make a crusade more just than this of ours. We were patient, too long patient, perhaps, with challenges. We seek no conquest. We fight to protect the freedom of our citizens. On America's standard is written democracy, on that of Germany autocracy. Without reservation women can give their all to attain our end.

There may be a cleavage between the German people and the ruling class. It may be that our foe is merely the military caste, though I am inclined to believe that we have the entire German nation on our hands. The supremacy of might may be a doctrine merely instilled in the minds of the people by its rulers. Perhaps the weed is not indigenous, but it flourishes, nevertheless. Rabbits did not belong in Australia, nor pondweed in England, but there they are, and dominating the situation. Arrogance of the strong towards the weak, of the better placed towards the less well placed, is part of the government teaching in Germany. The peasant woman harries the dog that strains at the market cart, her husband harries her as she helps the cow drag the plough, the petty officer harries the peasant when he is a raw recruit, and the young lieutenant harries the petty officer, and so it goes up to the highest,--a well-planned system on the part of the superior to bring the inferior to a high point of material efficiency. The propelling spirit is devotion to the Fatherland: each believes himself a cog in the machine chosen of God to achieve His purposes on earth. The world hears of the Kaiser's "Ich und Gott," of his mailed fist beating down his enemies, but those who have lived in Germany know that exactly the same spirit reigns in every class. The strong in chastizing his inferior has the conviction that since might makes right he is the direct representative of Deity on the particular occasion.

The overbearing spirit of the Prussian military caste has drilled a race to worship might; men are overbearing towards women, women towards children, and the laws reflect the cruelties of the strong towards the weak.

As the recent petition of German suffragists to the Reichstag states, their country stands "in the lowest rank of nations as regards women's rights." It is a platitude just now worth repeating that the civilization of a people is indicated by the position accorded to its women. On that head, then, the Teutonic Kultur stands challenged.

An English friend of mine threw down the gauntlet thirty years ago. She had married a German officer. After living at army posts all over the Empire, she declared, "What we foreigners take as simple childlikeness in the Germans is merely lack of civilization." This keen analysis came from a woman trained as an investigator, and equipped with perfect command of the language of her adopted country.

"Lack of civilization,"--perhaps that explains my having seen again and again officers striking the soldiers they were drilling, and journeys made torture through witnessing slapping and brow-beating of children by their parents. The memory of a father's conduct towards his little son will never be wiped out. He twisted the child's arm, struck him savagely from time to time, and for no reason but that the child did not sit bolt upright and keep absolutely motionless. The witnesses of the brutality smiled approvingly at the man, and scowled at the child. My own protest being met with amazed silence and in no way regarded, I left the compartment. I was near Eisenach, and I wished some good fairy would put in my hand that inkpot which Luther threw at the devil. Severity towards children is the rule. The child for weal or woe is in the complete control of its parents, and corporal punishment is allowed in the schools. The grim saying, "Saure Wochen, frohe Feste," seems to express the pedagogic philosophy. The only trouble is that nature does not give this attitude her sanction, for Germany reveals to us that figure, the most pathetic in life, the child suicide.

The man responding to his stern upbringing is in turn cruel to his inferiors, and full of subterfuge in dealing with equals. He is at home in the intrigues which have startled the world. In such a society the frank and gentle go to the wall, or--get into trouble and emigrate. We have profited--let us not forget it--by the plucky German immigrants who threw off the yoke, and who now have the satisfaction of finding themselves fighting shoulder to shoulder with the men of their adopted country to free the Fatherland of the taskmaster.

The philosophy of might quite naturally reflects itself in the education of girls. Once when I visited a Höhere Töchter Schule, the principal had a class in geometry recite for my edification. I soon saw that the young girl who had been chosen as the star pupil to wrestle with the pons asinorum was giving an exhibition of memorizing and not of mathematical reasoning. I asked the principal if my surmise were correct. He replied without hesitation, "Yes, it was entirely a feat in memory. Females have only low reasoning power." I urged that if this were so, it would be well to train the faculty, but he countered with the assertion, "We Germans do not think so. Women are happier and more useful without logic."

It would be difficult to surpass in its subtle cruelty the etiquette at a military function. The lieutenant and his wife come early,--this is expected of them. For a few moments they play the role of honored guests. The wife is shown by her hostess to the sofa and is seated there as a mark of distinction. Then arrive the captain and his wife. They are immediately the distinguished guests. The wife is shown to the sofa and the lieutenant's little Frau must get herself out of the way as best she can.

My speculation, often indulged in, as to what would happen if the major's wife did not move from the sofa when the colonel's wife appeared, ended in assurance that a severe punishment would be meted out to her, when I heard from an officer the story of the way his regiment dealt with a woman who ignored another bit of military etiquette. A débutant, once honored by being asked to dance with an officer at a ball, must never, it seems, demean herself by accepting a civilian partner. But in a town where my friend's regiment was stationed a very pretty and popular young girl who had been taken, so to speak, to the bosom of the regiment, danced one night at the Kurhaus early in the summer season with a civilian, distinguished, undeniably, but unmistakably civilian. The officers of the regiment met, weighed the mighty question of the girl's offense, and solemnly resolved never again to ask the culprit for a dance. I protested at the cruelty of a body of men deliberately turning a pretty young thing into a wall-flower for an entire season. The officer took my protest as an added reason for congratulation upon their conduct. They meant to be cruel. My words proved how well they had succeeded.

Another little straw showing the set of the wind: we were sitting, four Americans, one lovely early summer day, in a restaurant at Swinemünde. We had the window open, looking out over the sea. At the next table were some officers, one of whom with an "Es zieht," but not with a "by your leave," came over to our table and shut the window with a bang. The gentleman with us asked if we wanted the window closed, and on being assured we did not, quietly rose and opened it again. No one who does not know Prussia can imagine the threatening atmosphere which filled that café.

We met the officers the same night at the Kurhaus dance. They were introduced, and almost immediately one of them brought up the window incident and said most impressively that if ladies had not been at the table, our escort would have been "called out." We could see they regarded us as unworthy of being even transient participants of Kultur when we opined that no American man would accept a challenge, and if so unwise as to do so, his womenfolk would lock him up until he reached a sounder judgment! The swords rattled in their sabres when the frivolous member of our party said with a tone of finality, "You see we wouldn't like our men's faces to look as if they had got into their mothers' chopping bowls!"

Although I had often lived months on end with all these petty tyrannies of the mailed fist, and although life had taught me later that peoples grow by what they feed upon, yet when I read the Bryce report,[1] German frightfulness seemed too inhuman for belief. While still holding my judgment in reserve, I met an intimate friend, a Prussian officer. He happened to mention letters he had received from his relatives in Berlin and at the front, and when I expressed a wish to hear them, kindly asked whether he should translate them or read them in German as they stood. Laughingly I ventured on the German, saying I would at least find out how much I had forgotten. So I sat and listened with ears pricked up. Some of the letters were from women folk and told of war conditions in the capital. They were interesting at the time but not worth repeating now. Then came a letter from a nephew, a lieutenant. He gave his experience in crossing Belgium, told how in one village his men asked a young woman with her tiny baby on her arm for water, how she answered resentfully, and then, how he shot her--and her baby. I exclaimed, thinking I had lost the thread of the letter, "Not the baby?" And the man I supposed I knew as civilized, replied with a cruel smile, "Yes--discipline!" That was frank, frank as a child would have been, with no realization of the self-revelation of it. The young officer did the deed, wrote of it to his uncle, and the uncle, without vision and understanding, perverted by his training, did not feel shame and bury the secret in his own heart, but treasured the evidence against his own nephew, and laid it open before an American woman.

I believed the Bryce report--every word of it!

And I hate the system that has so bent and crippled a great race. Revenge we must not feel, that would be to innoculate ourselves with the enemy's virus. But let us be awake to the fact that might making right cuts athwart our ideals. German Kultur, through worship of efficiency, cramps originality and initiative, while our aim--why not be frank about it!--is the protection of inefficiency, which means sympathy with childhood, and opportunity for the spirit of art. German Kultur fixes an inflexible limit to the aspirations of women, while our goal is complete freedom for the mothers of men.

The women of the Allies can fight for all that their men fight for--for national self-respect, for protection of citizens, for the sacredness of international agreements, for the rights of small nations, for the security of democracy, and then our women can be inspired by one thing more--the safety and development of all those things which they have won for human welfare in a long and bloodless battle.

Women fight for a place in the sun for those who hold right above might.

[1] Report of the Committee on Alleged German Outrages appointed by his Britannic Majesty's Government. 1915. Macmillan Company, New York.

Evidence and Documents laid before the Committee on Alleged German Outrages. Ballantyne, Hanson & Co., London. 1915.

II
WINNING THE WAR

The group of nations that can make the greatest savings, will be victorious, counsels one; the group that can produce the most food and nourish the populations best, will win the war, urges another; but whatever the prophecy, whatever the advice, all paths to victory lie through labor-power.

Needs are not answered in our day by manna dropping from heaven. Whether it is food or big guns that are wanted, ships or coal, we can only get our heart's desire by toil. Where are the workers who will win the war?

We are a bit spoiled in the United States. We have been accustomed to rub our Aladdin's lamp of opportunity and the good genii have sent us workers. But suddenly, no matter how great our efforts, no one answers our appeal. The reservoir of immigrant labor has run dry. We are in sorry plight, for we have suffered from emigration, too. Thousands of alien workers have been called back to serve in the armies of the Allies. In my own little village on Long Island the industrious Italian colony was broken up by the call to return to the colors in Piedmont.

Then, too, while Europe suffers loss of labor, as do we, when men are mobilized, our situation is peculiarly poignant, for when our armies are gone they are gone. At first this was true in Europe. Men entered the army and were employed as soldiers only. After a time it was realized that the war would not be short, that fields must not lie untilled for years, nor men undergo the deteriorating effects of trench warfare continuously. The fallow field and the stale soldier were brought together.

We have all chanced on photographs of European soldiers helping the women plough in springtime, and reap the harvest in the autumn. Perhaps we have regarded the scene as a mere pastoral episode in a happy leave from the battle front, instead of realizing that it is a snapshot illustrating a well organized plan of securing labor. The soldiers are given a furlough and are sent where the agricultural need is pressing. But the American soldier will not be able to lend his skill in giving the home fields a rich seed time and harvest. The two needs, the field for the touch of the human hand, and the soldier for labor under calm skies, cannot in our case be coördinated.

Scarcity of labor is not only certain to grow, but the demands upon the United States for service are increasing by leaps and bounds. America must throw man-power into the trenches, must feed herself, must contribute more and ever more food to the hungry populations of Europe, must meet the old industrial obligations, and respond to a whole range of new business requirements. And she is called upon for this effort at a time when national prosperity is already making full use of man-power.

When Europe went to war, the world had been suffering from depression a year and more. Immediately on the outbreak of hostilities whole lines of business shut down. Unemployment became serious. There were idle hands everywhere. Germany, of all the belligerents, rallied most quickly to meet war conditions. Unemployment gave place to a shortage of labor sooner there than elsewhere. Great Britain did not begin to get the pace until the middle of 1915.

The business situation in the United States upon its entrance into the war was the antithesis of this. For over a year, depression had been superseded by increased industry, high wages, and greater demand for labor. The country as measured by the ordinary financial signs, by its commerce, by its labor market, was more prosperous than it had been for years. Tremendous requisitions were being made upon us by Europe, and to the limit of available labor we were answering them. Then into our economic life, with industrial forces already working at high pressure, were injected the new demands arising from changing the United States from a people as unprepared for effective hostilities as a baby in its cradle, into a nation equipped for war. There was no unemployment, but on the contrary, shortage of labor.

The country calls for everything, and all at once, like the spoiled child on suddenly waking. It must have, and without delay, ships, coal, cars, cantonments, uniforms, rules, and food, food, food. How can the needs be supplied and with a million and a half of men dropping work besides? By woman-power or coolie labor. Those are the horns of the dilemma presented to puzzled America. The Senate of the United States directs its Committee of Agriculture to ponder well the coolie problem, for men hesitate to have women put their shoulder to the wheel. Trade unionists are right in urging that a republic has no place for a disfranchised class of imported toilers. Equally true is it that as a nation we have shown no gift for dealing with less developed races. And yet labor we must have. Will American women supply it, will they, loving ease, favor contract labor from the outside, or will they accept the optimistic view that lack of labor is not acute?

The procrastinator queries, "Cannot American man-power meet the demand?" It can, for a time perhaps, if the draft for the army goes as slowly in the future as it has in the past.

However, at any moment a full realization may come to us of the significance of the fact that while the United States is putting only three percent of its workers into the fighting forces, Great Britain has put twenty-five percent, and is now combing its industrial army over to find an additional five hundred thousand men to throw on the French front. It is probable that it will be felt by this country in the near future that such a contrast of fulfillment of obligation cannot continue without serious reflection on our national honor. Roughly speaking, Great Britain has twenty million persons in gainful pursuits. Of these, five million have already been taken for the army. The contribution of France is still greater. Her military force has reached the appalling proportion of one-fifth of her entire population. But we who have thirty-five million in gainful occupations are giving a paltry one million, five hundred thousand in service with our Allies. The situation is not creditable to us, and one of the things which stands in the way of the United States reaching a more worthy position is reluctance to see its women shouldering economic burdens.

They wear the uniforms of the Edinburgh trams and the New York City subway and trolley guards, with pride and purpose.

While it is quite true that shifting of man-power is needed, mere shuffling of the cards, as labor leaders suggest, won't give a bigger pack. Fifty-two cards it remains, though the Jack may be put into a more suitable position. The man behind the counter should of course be moved to a muscular employment, but we must not interpret his dalliance with tapes and ribbons as proof of a superfluity of men.

The latest reports of the New York State Department of Labor reflect the meagerness of the supply. Here are some dull figures to prove it:-- comparing the situation with a year ago, we find in a corresponding month, only one percent more employees this year, with a wage advance of seventeen percent. Drawing the comparison between this year and two years ago, there is an advance of "fifteen percent in employees and fifty-one percent in wages;" and an increase of "thirty percent in employees and eighty-seven percent in wages," if this year is compared with the conditions when the world was suffering from industrial depression. The State employment offices report eight thousand three hundred and seventy-six requests for workers against seven thousand, six hundred and fifty applicants for employment, and of the latter only seventy-three percent were fitted for the grades of work open to them, and were placed in situations.

The last records of conditions in the Wilkes-Barre coal regions confirm the fact of labor scarcity. There are one hundred and fifty-two thousand men and boys at work today in the anthracite fields, twenty-five thousand less than the number employed in 1916. These miners, owing to the prod of the highest wages ever received--the skilled man earning from forty dollars to seventy-five dollars a week--and to appeals to their patriotism, are individually producing a larger output than ever before. It is considered that production, with the present labor force, is at its maximum, and if a yield of coal commensurate with the world's need is to be attained, at least seventy percent more men must be supplied.

This is a call for man-power in addition to that suggested by the Fuel Administrator to the effect that lack of coal is partly lack of cars and that "back of the transportation shortage lies labor shortage." An order was sent out by the Director General of Railways, soon after his appointment, that mechanics from the repair shops of the west were to be shifted to the east to supply the call for help on the Atlantic border.

Suggestive of the cause of all this shortage, float the service flags of the mining and railway companies, the hundreds of glowing stars telling their tale of men gone to the front, and of just so many stars torn from the standards of the industrial army at home.

The Shipping Board recently called for two hundred and fifty thousand men to be gradually recruited as a skilled army for work in shipyards. At the same time the Congress passed an appropriation of fifty million dollars for building houses to accommodate ship labor. Six months ago only fifty thousand men were employed in ship-building, today there are one hundred and forty-five thousand. This rapid drawing of men to new centers creates a housing problem so huge that it must he met by the government; and it need hardly be pointed out, shelter can be built only by human hands.

One state official, prompted no doubt by a wise hostility to coolie labor, and dread of woman labor, has gone so far as to declare publicly that any employer who will pay "adequate wages can get all the labor he requires." This view suggests that we may soon have to adopt the methods of other belligerents and stop employers by law from stealing a neighbor's working force. I know of a shipyard with a normal pay-roll of five hundred hands, which in one year engaged and lost to nearby munition factories thirteen thousand laborers. Such "shifting," hiding as it does shortage of manpower, leads to serious loss in our productive efficiency and should not be allowed to go unchecked.

The manager of one of the New York City street railways met with complete denial the easy optimism that adequate remuneration will command a sufficient supply of men. He told me that he had introduced women at the same wage as male conductors, not because he wanted women, but because he now had only five applications by fit men to thirty or forty formerly. There were men to be had, he said, and at lower wages than his company was paying; but they were "not of the class capable of fulfilling the requirements of the position."

The Labor Administration announced on its creation that its "policy would be to prevent woman labor in positions for which men are available," and one of the deputy commissioners of the Industrial Commission of the State of New York declared quite frankly at a labor conference that "if he could, he would exclude women from industry altogether."

We may try to prevent the oncoming tide of the economic independence of women, but it will not be possible to force the business world to accept permanently the service of the inefficient in place of that of the alert and intelligent. To carry on the economic life of a nation with its labor flotsam and jetsam is loss at any time; in time of storm and stress it is suicide.

Man-power is short, seriously so. The farm is always the best barometer to give warning of scarcity of labor. The land has been drained of its workers. A fair wage would keep them on the farm--this is the philosophy of laissez faire. Without stopping to inquire as to what the munition works would then do, we can still see that it is doubtful whether the farm can act as magnet. Even men, let us venture the suggestion, like change for the mere sake of change. A middle-aged man, who had taken up work at Bridgeport, said to me, "I've mulled around on the farm all my days. I grabbed the first chance to get away." And then there's a finer spirit prompting the desertion of the hoe. A man of thirty-three gave me the point of view. "My brother is 'over there,' and I feel as if I were backing him up by making guns."

The only thing that can change the idea that farming is "mulling around," and making a gun "backs up" the man at the front more thoroughly than raising turnips, is to bring to the farm new workers who realize the vital part played by food in the winning of the war. As the modern industrial system has developed with its marvels of specialized machinery, its army of employees gathered and dispersed on the stroke of the clock, and strong organizations created to protect the interests of the worker, the calm and quiet processes of agriculture have in comparison grown colorless. The average farmhand has never found push and drive and group action on the farm, but only individualism to the extreme of isolation. And now in war time, when in addition to its usual life of stirring contacts, the factory takes on an intimate and striking relation to the intense experience of the battle front, the work of the farm seems as flat as it is likely to be unprofitable. The man in the furrow has no idea that he is "backing up" the boy in the trench.

The farmer in his turn does not find himself part of the wider relations that attract and support the manufacturer. Crops are not grown on order. The marketing is as uncertain as the weather. The farmer could by higher wages attract more labor, but as the selling of the harvest remains a haphazard matter, the venture might mean ruin all the more certain and serious were wage outlay large. In response to a call for food and an appeal to his patriotism, the farmer has repeatedly made unusual efforts to bring his land to the maximum fertility, only to find his crops often a dead loss, as he could not secure the labor to harvest them. I saw, one summer, acres of garden truck at its prime ploughed under in Connecticut because of a shortage of labor. I saw fruit left rotting by the bushel in the orchards near

Rochester because of scarcity of pickers and a doubt of the reliability of the market. The industry which means more than any other to the well-being of humanity at this crisis, is the sport of methods outgrown and of servants who lack understanding and inspiration. The war may furnish the spark for the needed revolution. Man-power is not available, woman-power is at hand. A new labor force always brings ideas and ideals peculiar to itself. May not women as fresh recruits in a land army stamp their likes and dislikes on farm life? Their enthusiasm may put staleness to rout, and the group system of women land workers, already tested in the crucible of experience, may bring to the farm the needed antidote to isolation.

To win the war we must have man-power in the trenches sufficient to win it with. To win, every soldier, every sailor, must be well fed, well clothed, well equipped. To win, behind the armed forces must stand determined peoples. To win, the people of America and her Allies must be heartened by care and food.

The sun shines on the fertile land, the earth teems with forests, with coal, with every necessary mineral and food, but labor, labor alone can transform all to meet our necessities. Man-power unaided cannot supply the demand. Women in America must shoulder as nobly as have the women of Europe, this duty. They must answer their country's call. Let them see clearly that the desire of their men to shield them from possible injury exposes the nation and the world to actual danger.

Our winning of the war depends upon the full use of the energy of our entire people. Every muscle, every brain, must be mobilized if the national aim is to be achieved.

III
MOBILIZING WOMEN IN GREAT
BRITAIN [2]

In no country have women reached a mobilization so complete and systematized as in Great Britain. This mobilization covers the whole field of war service--in industry, business and professional life, and in government administration. Women serve on the Ministry of Food and are included in the membership of twenty-five of the important government committees, not auxiliary or advisory, but administrative committees, such as those on War Pensions, on Disabled Officers and Men, on Education after the War, and the Labor Commission to Deal with Industrial Unrest.

In short, the women of Great Britain are working side by side with men in the initiation and execution of plans to solve the problems which confront the nation.

Four committees, as for instance those making investigations and recommendations on Women's Wages and Drink Among Women, are entirely composed of women, and great departments, such as the Women's Land Army, the Women's Army Auxiliary Corps, are officered throughout by them. Hospitals under the War Office have been placed in complete control of medical women; they take rank with medical men in the army and receive the pay going with their commissions.

When Great Britain recognized that the war could not be won by merely sending splendid fighters to the front and meeting the wastage by steady drafts upon the manhood of the country, she began to build an efficient organization of industry at home.

To the call for labor-power British women gave instant response. In munitions a million are mobilized, in the Land Army there have been drafted and actually placed on the farms over three hundred thousand, and in the Women's Army Auxiliary Corps fourteen thousand women are working in direct connection with the fighting force, and an additional ten thousand are being called out for service each month. In the clerical force of the government departments, some of which had never seen women before in their sacred precincts, over one hundred and ninety-eight thousand are now working. And the women civil servants are not only engaged in indoor service, but outside too, most of the carrying of mail being in their hands.

Women are dock-laborers, some seven thousand strong. Four thousand act as patrols and police, forty thousand are in banks and various financial houses. It is said that there are in Great Britain scarce a million women--and they are mostly occupied as housewives--who could render greater service to their country than that which they are now giving.

The wide inclusion of women in government administration is very striking to us in America. But we must not forget that the contrast between the two countries in the participation of women in political life and public service has always been great. The women of the United Kingdom have enjoyed the municipal and county franchise for years. For a long time large numbers of women have been called to administrative positions. They have had thorough training in government as Poor Law Guardians, District and County Councilors, members of School Boards. No women, the whole world over, are equipped as those of Great Britain for service to the state.

In the glamor of the extremely striking government service of British women, we must not overlook their non-official organizations. Perhaps these offer the most valuable suggestions for America. They are near enough to our experience to be quite understandable.

The mother country is not under regimentation. Originality and initiative have full play. Perhaps it was well that the government failed to appreciate what women could do, and neglected them so long. Most of the effective work was started in volunteer societies and had proved a success before there was an official laying on of hands. Anglo-Saxons--it is our strong point--always work from below, up.

A glance at any account of the mobilization of woman-power in Great Britain, Miss Fraser's admirable "Women and War Work," for instance, will reveal the printed page dotted thick with the names of volunteer associations. A woman with sympathy sees a need, she gets an idea and calls others about her. Quickly, there being no red tape, the need begins to be met. What more admirable service could have been performed than that inaugurated in the early months of the war under the Queen's Work for Women Fund, when work was secured for the women in luxury trades which were collapsing under war pressure? A hundred and thirty firms employing women were kept running.

What more thrilling example of courage and forethought has been shown than by the Scottish Women's Hospitals in putting on the western front the first X-ray car to move from point to point near the lines? It but adds to the appeal of the work that those great scientists, Mrs. Ayrton and Madame Curie, selected the equipment.

It was a non-official body, the National Union of Women's Suffrage Societies, which opened before the war was two weeks old the Women's Service Bureau, and soon placed forty thousand women as paid and volunteer workers. It was this bureau that furnished the government with its supervisors for the arsenals. The Women's Farm and Garden Union was the fore-runner of the official Land Army, and to it still is left the important work of enrolling those women who, while willing to undertake agricultural work, are disinclined to sign up for service "for the duration of the war."

Not only have unnumbered voluntary associations achieved miracles in necessary work, but many of them have gained untold discipline in the ridicule they have had to endure from a doubting public. I remember hunting in vain all about Oxford Circus for the tucked-away office of the Women's Signalling Corps. My inquiries only made the London bobbies grin. Everyone laughed at the idea of women signalling, but to-day the members are recognized officially, one holding an important appointment in the college of wireless telegraphy.

How Scotland Yard smiled, at first, at Miss Damer Dawson and her Women Police Service! But now the metropolitan police are calling for the help of her splendidly trained and reliable force.

And the Women's Reserve Ambulance Corps--I climbed and climbed to an attic to visit their headquarters! There was the commandant in her khaki, very gracious, but very upstanding, and maintaining the strictest discipline. No member of the corps entered or left her office without clapping heels together and saluting. The ambulance about which the corps revolved, I often met in the streets--empty. But those women had vision. They saw that England would need them some day. They had faith in their ability to serve. So on and on they went, training themselves to higher efficiency in body and mind. And to-day--well, theirs is always the first ambulance on the spot to care for the injured in the air-raids. The scoffers have remained to pray.

If Britain has a lesson for us it is an all-hail to non-official societies, an encouragement to every idea, a blessing on every effort which has behind it honesty of purpose. Great Britain's activities are as refreshingly diversified as her talents. They are not all under one hat.

In the training for new industrial openings this same spirit of non-official service showed itself. In munitions, for instance, private employers were the first to recognize that they had in women-workers a labor force worth the cost of training. The best of the skilled men in many cases were told off to give the necessary instruction. The will to do was in the learner; she soon mastered even complex processes, and at the end of a few weeks was doing even better than men in the light work, and achieving commendable output in the heavy. The suffrage organizations, whenever a new line of skilled work was opened to women, established well-equipped centers to give the necessary teaching. Not until it became apparent that the new labor-power only needed training to reach a high grade of proficiency, did County Councils establish, at government expense, technical classes for girls and women.

Then--the offered service of the Women's Reserve Ambulance Corps in England was spurned. Now--they wear shrapnel helmets while working during the Zeppelin raids.

Equipment of the army was obviously the first and pressing obligation. Fields might lie fallow, for food in the early days could easily be brought from abroad, but men had to be registered, soldiers clothed and equipped. It was natural, then, that the new workers were principally used in registration work and in making military supplies.

But in the second year of the war came the conviction that the contest was not soon to be ended, and that the matter of raising food at home must be met. Women were again appealed to. A Land Army mobilized by women was created. At first this work was carried on under a centralized division of the National Service Department, but there has been decentralization and the Land Army is now a department of the Board of Agriculture. It is headed by Miss M. Talbot as director. Under this central body are Women's Agricultural Committees in each county, with an organizing secretary whose duty it is to secure full-time recruits.

The part-time workers in a locality are obtained by the wife of the squire or vicar acting as a volunteer registrar. Many of these part-time workers register to do the domestic work of the lusty young village housewife or mother while she is absent from home performing her allotted task on a nearby farm. The full-time recruits are not only secured by the organizers, but through registrations at every post office. Any woman can ask for a registration card and fill it out, and the postmaster then forwards the application to the committee. The next step is that likely applicants are called to the nearest center for examination and presentation of credentials. When finally accepted they are usually sent for six weeks' or three months' training to a farm belonging to some large estate. The landlord contributes the training, and the government gives the recruit her uniform and fifteen shillings a week to cover her board and lodging. At the end of her course she receives an armlet signifying her rank in the Land Army and is ready to go wherever the authorities send her.

The farmer in Great Britain no longer needs to be converted to the value of the new workers. He knows they can do every kind of farm work as well as men, and are more reliable and conscientious than boys, and he is ready, therefore, to pay the required minimum wage of eighteen shillings a week, or above that amount if the rate ruling in the district is higher.

Equally well organized is the Women's Army Auxiliary Corps, familiarly known as the Waacs. The director is Mrs. Chalmers Watson. A would-be Waac goes to the center in her county for examination, and then is assigned to work at home or "somewhere in France" according to training and capacity. She may be fitted as a cook, a storekeeper, a telephone or telegraph operator, or for signalling or salvage work. Let us not say she will supplant a man, but rather set a man free for fuller service.

My niece, a slip of a girl, felt the call of duty at the beginning of the war. Her brothers were early volunteers in Kitchener's Army. They were in the trenches and she longed for the sensation of bearing a burden of hard work. She went to Woolwich Arsenal and toiled twelve hours a day. She broke under the strain, recuperated, and took up munition work again. She became expert, and was in time an overseer told off to train other women. But she was never satisfied, and always anxious to be nearer the great struggle. She broke away one day and went to Southampton for a Waac examination, and found herself one of a group of a hundred and fifty gentlewomen all anxious to enter active service and all prepared for some definite work. They stood their tests, and Dolly--that's the little niece's pet name, given to her because she is so tiny--is now working as an "engine fitter" just behind the fighting lines. Dainty Dolly, whom we have always treated as a fragile bit of Sèvres china, clad in breeches and puttees, under the booming of the great guns, is fitting patiently, part to part, the beating engine which will lift on wings some English boy in his flight through the blue skies of France.

But it must not be supposed that the magnificent service of British women, devoted, efficient and well-organized from top to bottom, realized itself without friction, any more than it will here. There were certainly two wars going on in Great Britain for a long time, and the internal strife was little less bitter than the international conflict. The most active center of this contest of which we have heard so little was in industry, and the combatants were the government, trade unions and women. The unions were doing battle because of fear of unskilled workers, especially when intelligent and easily trained; the government, in sore need of munition hands, was bargaining with the unskilled for long hours and low pay. Finally the government and the unions reluctantly agreed that women must be employed; both wanted them to be skillful, but not too skillful, and above all, to remain amenable. It has been made clear, too, that women enter their new positions "for the war only." At the end of hostilities--international hostilities-- women are to hand over their work and wages to men and go home and be content. Will the program be fulfilled?

The wishes of women themselves may play some part. How do they feel? Obviously, every day the war lasts they get wider experience of the sorrows and pleasures of financial independence. Women are called the practical sex, and I certainly found them in England facing the fact that peace will mean an insufficient number of breadwinners to go around and that a maimed man may have low earning power. The women I met were not dejected at the prospect; they showed, on the contrary, a spirit not far removed from elation in finding new opportunities of service. After I had sat and listened to speech after speech at the annual conference of the National Union of Women Workers, with delegates from all parts of the country, presided over by Mrs. Creighton, widow of the late Bishop of London, there was no doubt in my mind that British women desired to enter paid fields of work, and regarded as permanent the great increase in their employment. No regrets or hesitations were expressed in a single speech, and the solutions of the problems inherent in the new situation all lay in the direction of equality of preparation and equality of pay with men.

The strongest element in the women's trade unions takes the same stand. The great rise in the employment of women is not regarded as a "war measure," and all the suggestions made to meet the hardships of readjustment, such as a "minimum wage for all unskilled workers, men as well as women," are based on the idea of the new workers being permanent factors in the labor market.

The same conclusion was reached in the report presented to the British Association by the committee appointed to investigate the "Replacement of Male by Female Labor." The committee found itself in entire disagreement with the opinion that the increased employment of women was a passing phase, and made recommendations bearing on such measures as improved technical training for girls as well as for boys, a minimum wage for unskilled men as well as women, equal pay for equal work, and the abolition of "half-timers." But while it was obvious that the greatest asset of belligerent nations is the labor of women, while learned societies and organizations of women laid down rules for their safe and permanent employment, the British Government showed marked opposition to the new workers. If the Cabinet did not believe the war would be brief, it certainly acted as if Great Britain alone among the belligerents would have no shortage of male industrial hands. At a time when Germany had five hundred thousand women in munition factories, England had but ten thousand.

There is no doubt that the country was at first organized merely for a spurt. Boys and girls were pressed into service, wages were cut down for women, hours lengthened for men. Government reports read like the Shaftesbury attacks on the conditions of early factory days. We hear again of beds that are never cold, the occupant of one shift succeeding the occupant of the next, of the boy sleeping in the same bed with two men, and three girls in a cot in the same room. Labor unrest was met at first by the Munitions War Act prohibiting strikes and lockouts, establishing compulsory arbitration and suspending all trade-union rules which might "hamper production." Under the law a "voluntary army of workers" signed up as ready to go anywhere their labor was needed, and local munition committees became labor courts endowed with power to change wage rates, to inflict fines on slackers, and on those who broke the agreements of the "voluntary army."

To meet the threatening rebellion, a Health of Munition Workers Committee under the Ministry of Munitions was appointed to "consider and advise on questions of industrial fatigue, hours of labor and other matters affecting the physical health and physical efficiency of workers in munition factories and workshops." On this committee there were distinguished medical men, labor experts, members of parliament and two women, Miss R.E. Squire of the Factory Department and Mrs. H.J. Tennant.

The committee was guided by a desire to have immense quantities of munitions turned out, and faced squarely the probability that the war would be of long duration. Its findings, embodied in a series of memoranda, have lessons for us, not only for war times, but for peace times, for all time.

On a seven day week the verdict was that "if the maximum output is to be secured and maintained for any length of time, a weekly period of rest must be allowed." Overtime was advised against, a double or triple shift being recommended.

In July, 1916, the committee published a most interesting memorandum on experiments in the relation of output to hours. In one case the output was increased eight percent by reducing the weekly hours from sixty-eight to fifty-nine, and it was found that a decrease to fifty-six hours per week gave the same output as fifty-nine. It need hardly be said that there was no change in machinery, tools, raw material or workers. All elements except hours of work were identical. Twenty-seven workers doing very heavy work increased their output ten percent by cutting weekly hours from sixty-one to fifty-five. In a munition plant employing thirty-six thousand hands it was found that the sick rate ranged from five to eight percent when the employees were working overtime, and was only three percent when they were on a double shift.

The war has forced Great Britain to carry out the findings of this committee and to consider more seriously than ever before, and for both men and women, the problem of industrial fatigue, the relation of accidents to hours of labor, industrial diseases, housing, transit, and industrial canteens. The munition worker is as important as the soldier and must have the best of care.

While the friction in the ranks of industrial women workers was still far from being adjusted, the government met its Waterloo in the contest with medical women. The service which they freely offered their country was at first sternly refused. Undaunted, they sought recognition outside the mother country. They knew their skill and they knew the soldiers' need. They turned to hospitable France, and received official recognition. On December 14, 1914, the first hospital at the front under British medical women was opened in Abbaye Royaumont, near Creil. It carries the official designation, "Hôpital Auxiliaire 301." The doctors, the nurses, the cooks, are all women. One of the capable chauffeurs I saw running the ambulance when I was in Creil. She was getting the wounded as they came down from the front. The French Government appreciated what the women were doing and urged them to give more help. At Troyes another unit gave the French army its first experience of nursing under canvas.

After France had been profiting by the skill of British women for months, Sir Alfred Keogh, Medical Director General, wisely insisted that the War Office yield and place a hospital in the hands of women. The War Hospital in Endell Street, London, is now under Dr. Flora Murray, and every office, except that of gateman, is filled by women. From the doctors, who rank as majors, down to the cooks, who rank as non-commissioned officers, every one connected with Endell Street has military standing. It indicated the long, hard road these women had traveled to secure official recognition that the doctor who showed me over the hospital told me, as a matter for congratulation, that at night the police brought in drunken soldiers to be sobered. "Every war hospital must receive them," she explained, "and we are glad we are not passed over, for that gives the stamp to our official standing."

It was a beautiful autumn day when I visited Endell Street. The great court was full of convalescents, and the orderlies in khaki, with veils floating back from their close-fitting toques, were carefully and skillfully lifting the wounded from an ambulance. I spoke to one of the soldier boys about the absence of men doctors and orderlies, and his quick query was, "And what should we want men for?" It seems that they always take that stand after a day or two. At first the patient is puzzled; he calls the doctor "sister" and the orderly "nurse," but ends by being an enthusiastic champion of the new order. Not a misogynist did I find. One poor fellow who had been wounded again and again and had been in many hospitals, declared, "I don't mean no flattery, but this place leaves nothink wanting."

The first woman I met on my last visit to England upset my expectation of finding that war pushed women back into primitive conditions of toil, crushed them under the idea that physical force rules the world, and made them subservient. I chanced upon her as she was acting as ticket-puncher at the Yarmouth station. She was well set-up, alert, efficient, helpful in giving information, and, above all, cheerful. There were two capable young women at the bookstall, too. One had lost a brother at the front, the other her lover. I felt that they regarded their loss as one item in the big national accounting. They were heroically cheerful in "doing their bit."

Throughout my stay in England I searched for, but could not find, the self-effacing spinster of former days. In her place was a capable woman, bright-eyed, happy. She was occupied and bustled at her work. She jumped on and off moving vehicles with the alertness, if not the unconsciousness, of the expert male. She never let me stand in omnibus or subway, but quickly gave me her seat, as indeed she insisted upon doing for elderly gentlemen as well. The British woman had found herself and her muscles. England was a world of women-- women in uniforms; there was the army of nurses, and then the messengers, porters, elevator hands, tram conductors, bank clerks, bookkeepers, shop attendants. They each seemed to challenge the humble stranger, "Superfluous? Not I, I'm a recruit for national service!" Even a woman doing time-honored womanly work moved with an air of distinction; she dusted a room for the good of her country. Just one glimpse was I given of the old-time daughter of Eve, when a ticket-collector at Reading said: "I can't punch your ticket. Don't you see I'm eating an apple!"

One of the reactions of the wider functioning of brain and muscle which struck me most forcibly was the increased joyfulness of women. They were happy in their work, happy in the thought of rendering service, so happy that the poignancy of individual loss was carried more easily.

This cheerfulness is somewhat gruesomely voiced in a cartoon in *Punch* touching on the allowance given to the soldier's wife. She remarks, "This war is 'eaven--twenty-five shillings a week and no 'usband bothering about!" We have always credited *Punch* with knowing England. Truth stands revealed by a thrust, however cynical, when softened by challenging humor.

There was no discipline in the pension system. No work was required. The case of a girl I met in a country town was common. She was working in a factory earning eleven shillings a week. A day or two later I saw her, and she told me she had stopped work, as she had "married a soldier, and 'e's gone to France, and I get twelve and six separation allowance a week." Never did the strange English name, "separation allowance," seem more appropriate for the wife's pension than in this girl's story. Little wonder was it that in the early months of the war there was some riotous living among soldiers' wives!

And the comments of women of influence on the drunkenness and waste of money on foolish finery were as striking to me as the sordid condition itself. The woman chairman of a Board of Poor Law Guardians in the north of England told me that when her fellow-members suggested that Parliament ought to appoint committees to disburse the separation allowances, she opposed them with the heroic philosophy that women can be trained in wisdom only by freedom to err, that a sense of responsibility had never been cultivated in them, and the country would have to bear the consequences. In reply to my inquiry as to how the Guardians received these theories, I learned that "they knew she was right and dropped their plan."

The faith of leading women that experience would be the best teacher for the soldier's wife has been justified. A labor leader in the Midlands told me that an investigation by his trade union showed that only one hundred women in the ten thousand cases inquired into were mis-spending their allowances. And when I was visiting a board school in a poor district of London, and remarked to the head teacher that the children looked well cared for, she told me that never had they been so well fed and clothed. There seemed no doubt in her mind that it was best to have the family budget in the hands of the mother. In the sordid surroundings of the mean streets of great cities, there is developing in women practical wisdom and a fine sense of individual responsibility.

Perhaps of greater significance than just how separation allowances are being spent is the fact that women have discovered that their work as housewives and mothers has a value recognized by governments in hard cash. It makes one speculate as to whether wives in the warring nations will step back without a murmur into the old-time dependence on one man, or whether these simple women may contribute valuable ideas towards the working out of sound schemes of motherhood pensions.

The women of Great Britain are experiencing economic independence, they are living in an atmosphere of recognition of the value of their work as housewives and mothers. Women leaders in all classes give no indication of regarding pensions or remuneration in gainful pursuits as other than permanent factors in social development, and much of the best thought of men as well as women is centered on group experiments in domestic coöperation, in factory canteens, in municipal kitchens, which are a natural concomitant to the wider functioning of women.

Great Britain is not talking about feminism, it is living it. Perhaps nothing better illustrates the national acceptance of the fact than the widespread amusement touched with derision caused by the story of the choleric gentlemen who, on being asked at the time of one of the government registrations whether his wife was dependent upon him or not, roared in rage, "Well, if my wife isn't dependent on me, I'd like to know what man she is dependent on!"

Only second to Britain's lesson for us in the self-reliance of its women, and the thorough mobilization of their labor-power and executive ability, is its lesson in protection for all industrial workers. It stands as one people against the present enemy, and in its effort does not fail to give thought to race conservation for the future.

[2] Through the courtesy of the Editors of *The Outlook*, I am at liberty to use in this and the following chapter, some of the material published in an article by me in *The Outlook* of June 28, 1916.

IV
MOBILIZING WOMEN IN FRANCE

Compared with the friction in the mobilization of woman-power in Great Britain, the readjustment in the lives of women in France was like the opening out of some harmonious pageant in full accord with popular sympathy. But who has not said, "France is different!"

It is different, and in nothing more so than in its attitude toward its women. Without discussion with organizations of men, without hindrance from the government, women filled the gaps in the industrial army. It was obvious that the new workers, being unskilled, would need training; the government threw open the technical schools to them. A spirit of hospitality, of helpfulness, of common sense, reigned.

The French poilu on furlough is put to work harrowing.

And it was not only in industry that France showed herself wise. I found that the government had coöperated unreservedly with all the philanthropic work of women and had given them a wide sphere in which they could rise above amateurish effort and carry out plans calling for administrative ability.

When the Conseil National des Femmes Françaises inaugurated its work to bring together the scattered families of Belgium and northern France, and when the Association pour l'Aide Fraternelle aux Évacués Alsaciens-Lorrains began its work for the dispersed peoples of the provinces, an order was issued by the government to every prefect to furnish lists of all refugees in his district to the headquarters of the women's societies in Paris. It was through this good will on the part of the central government that these societies were able to bring together forty thousand Belgian families, and to clothe and place in school, or at work, the entire dispersed population of the reconquered districts of Alsace-Lorraine.

Nor did these societies cease work with the completion of their initial effort. They turned themselves into employment bureaus and with the aid and sanction of the government found work for the thousands of women who were thrown out of employment. They had the machinery to accomplish their object, the Council being an old established society organized throughout the country, and the Association to Aid the Refugees from Alsace-Lorraine (a nonpartisan name adopted, by the way, at the request of the Minister of the Interior to cover for the moment the patriotic work of the leading suffrage society) had active units in every prefecture.

One of the admirable private philanthropies was the canteen at the St. Lazarre station in Paris. I am tempted to single it out because its organizer, Countess de Berkaim, told me that in all the months she had been running it--and it was open twenty-four hours of the day--not a single volunteer had been five minutes late. The canteen was opened in February, 1915, with a reading and rest room. Six hundred soldiers a day have been fed. The two big rooms donated by the railway for the work were charming with their blue and white checked curtains, dividing kitchen from restaurant and rest room from reading room. The work is no small monument to the reliability and organizing faculty of French women.

It was in France, too, that I found the group of women who realized that the permanent change which the war was making in the relation of women to society needed fundamental handling. Mlle. Valentine Thomson, founder of La Vie Féminine, held that not only was the war an economic struggle and not only must the financial power of the combatants rest on the labor of women, but the future of the nations will largely depend upon the attitude which women take toward their new obligations. Realizing that business education would be a determining factor in that attitude, Mlle. Thomson persuaded her father, who was then Minister of Commerce, to send out an official recommendation to the Chambers of Commerce to open the commercial schools to girls. The advice was very generally followed, but as Paris refused, a group of women, backed by the Ministry, founded a school in which were given courses of instruction in the usual business subjects, and lectures on finance, commercial law and international trade.

Mlle. Thomson herself turned her business gifts to good use in a successful effort to build up for the immediate benefit of artists and workers the doll trade of which France was once supreme mistress. Exhibitions of the art, old and new, were held in many cities in the

United States, in South America and in England. The dolls went to the hearts of lovers of beauty, and what promised surer financial return, to the hearts of the children.

To do something for France--that stood first in the minds of the initiators of this commercial project. They knew her people must be employed. And next, the desire to bring back charm to an old art prompted their effort. Mlle. Thomson fully realizes just what "Made in Germany" signifies. The peoples of the world have had their taste corrupted by floods of the cheap and tawdry. Germany has been steadily educating us to demand quantity, quantity mountains high. There is promise that the doll at least will be rescued by France and made worth the child's devotion.

In industry, as well as in all else, one feels that in France there has not been so much a revolution as an orderly development. Women were in munition factories even before the war, the number has merely swelled. The women of the upper and lower bourgeois class always knew their husband's business, the one could manage the shop, the other could bargain with the best of them as to contracts and output. Women were trained as bookkeepers and clerks under Napoleon I; he wanted men as soldiers, and so decreed women should go into business. And the woman of the aristocratic class has merely slipped out of her seclusion as if putting aside an old-fashioned garment, and now carries on her philanthropies in more serious and coördinated manner.

We know the practical business experience possessed by French women, and so are prepared to learn that many a big commercial enterprise, the owner having gone to the front, is now directed by his capable wife. That is but a development, too, is it not? For we had all heard long ago of Mme. Duval, even if we had not eaten at her restaurants, and though we had never bought a ribbon or a carpet at the Bon Marché, we had heard of the woman who helped break through old merchant habits and gave the world the department store.

But nothing has been more significant in its growth during the war than the small enterprises in which the husband and wife in the domestic munition shop, laboring side by side with a little group of assistants, have been turning out marvels of skill. The man is now in the trenches fighting for France, and the woman takes command and leads the industrial battalion to victory. She knows she fights for France.

A word more about her business, for she is playing an economic part that brings us up at attention. She may be solving the problem of adjustment of home and work so puzzling to women. There are just such domestic shops dotted all over the map of France; in the Paris district alone there are over eighteen hundred of them. The conditions are so excellent and the ruling wages so high, that the minimum wage law passed in 1915 applied only to the sweated home workers in the clothing trade, and not to the domestic munition shops.

A commission which included in its membership a trade unionist, sent by the British government in the darkest days to find why it was that France could produce so much more ammunition than England, found these tiny workshops, with their primitive equipment, performing miracles. The output was huge and of the best. The woman, when at the head, seemed to turn out more than the man, she worked with such undying energy. The commission said it was the "spirit of France" that drove the workers forward and renewed the flagging energies. But even the trade unionist referred to the absence of all opposition to women on the part of organizations of men. Perhaps the spirit of France is undying because in it is a spirit of unity and harmony.

It seemed to me there was one very practical explanation of the unmistakable energy of the French worker, both man and woman. The whole nation has the wise custom of taking meal time with due seriousness. The break at noon in the great manufactories, as well as in the family workshop, is long, averaging one hour and a half, and reaching often to two hours. The French never gobble. Because food is necessary to animal life, they do not on that account take a puritanical view of it. They dare enjoy it, in spite of its physiological bearing. They sit down to it, dwell upon it, get its flavor, and after the meal they sit still and as a nation permit themselves unabashed to enjoy the sensation of hunger appeased. That's the common sense spirit of France.

Of course the worker is renewed, hurls herself on the work again with ardor, and losing no time through fatigue, throws off an enormous output.

Wages perform their material share in spurring the worker. Louis Barthou says that the woman's average is eight francs a day. Long ago--it seems long ago--she could earn at best five francs in the Paris district. She works on piece work now, getting the same rate as men. And think of it!--this must indeed be because of the spirit of France--this woman does better than men on the light munition work, and equals, yes, equals her menfolk on the heavy shells. I do not say this, a commission of men says it, a commission with a trade union member to boot. The coming of the woman-worker with the spirit of win-the-war in her heart is the same in France as elsewhere, only here her coming is more gracious. Twelve hundred easily take up work on the Paris subway. They are the wives of mobilized employees. The offices of the Post, the Telegraph and Telephone bristle with women, of course, for eleven thousand have taken the places of men. Some seven thousand fill up the empty positions on the railways, serving even as conductors on through trains. Their number has swollen to a half million in munitions, and to over half that number in powder mills and marine workshops; in civil establishments over three hundred thousand render service; and even the conservative banking world welcomes the help of some three thousand women.

Has there ever been anything impossible to French women since the time of Jeanne d'Arc? The fields must be harrowed--they have no horses.

Out on the land the tally is greatest of all. Every woman from the village bends over the bosom of France, urging fertility. The government called them in the first hours of the conflict. Viviani spoke the word:--

"The departure for the army of all those who can carry arms, leaves the work in the fields undone; the harvest is not yet gathered in; the vintage season is near. In the name of the entire nation united behind it, I make an appeal to your courage, and to that of your children, whose age alone and not their valour, keeps them from the war.

"I ask you to keep on the work in the fields, to finish gathering in the year's harvest, to prepare that of the coming year. You cannot render your country a greater service.

"It is not for you, but for her, that I appeal to your hearts.

"You must safeguard your own living, the feeding of the urban populations and especially the feeding of those who are defending the frontier, as well as the independence of the country, civilization and justice.

"Up, then, French women, young children, daughters and sons of the country! Replace on the field of work those who are on the field of battle. Strive to show them to-morrow the cultivated soil, the harvests all gathered in, the fields sown.

"In hours of stress like the present, there is no ignoble work. Everything that helps the country is great. Up! Act! To work! To-morrow there will be glory for everyone.

"Long live the Republic! Long live France!"

Women instantly responded to the proclamation. Only the old men were left to help, only decrepit horses, rejected by the military requisition. More than once I journeyed far into the country, but I never saw an able-bodied man. What a gap to be filled!--but the French peasant woman filled it. She harvested that first year, she has sowed and garnered season by season ever since. Men, horses, machinery were lacking, the debit yawned, but she piled up a credit to meet it by unflagging toil.

With equal devotion and with initiative and power of organization the woman of leisure has "carried on." The three great societies corresponding with our Red Cross, the Société de Secours aux Blessés, the Union des Femmes de France, and the Association des Dames Françaises, have established fifteen hundred hospitals with one hundred and fifteen thousand beds, and put forty-three thousand nurses in active service. Efficiency has kept pace with this superb effort, as is testified to by many a war cross, many a medal, and the cross of the Legion of Honor.

Up to the level of her means France sets examples in works of human salvage worthy the imitation of all nations. The mairie in each arrondissement has become no less than a community center. The XIV arrondissement in Paris is but the pattern for many. Here the wife of the mayor, Mme. Brunot, has made the stiff old building a human place. The card catalogue carrying information about every soldier from the district, gives its overwhelming news each day gently to wife or mother, through the lips of Mme. Brunot or her women assistants. The work of Les Amis des Orphelins de Guerre centers here, the "adopted" child receiving from the good maire the gifts in money and presents sent by the Americans who are generously filling the role of parent. The widows of the soldiers gather here for comfort and advice.

And the mairie holds a spirit of experiment. It houses not only courage and sympathy, but progress. The "XIV" has ventured on a Cuisine Populaire under Mme. Brunot's wholesome guidance. And so many other arrondissements have followed suit that Paris may be regarded as making a great experiment in the municipal feeding of her people. It is not charity, the food is paid for. In the "XIV" fifteen hundred persons eat a meal or two at the mairie each day. The charge is seventy-five centimes--fifteen cents, and one gets a soup, meat and a vegetable, and fruit.

The world seems to be counselling us that if we wish to be well and cheaply fed we must go where there are experts to cook, where buying is done in quantity, and where the manager knows about nutritive values.

If a word of praise is extended to the maire of the XIV arrondissement for his very splendid work, an example to all France, he quickly urges, "Ah, but Mme. Brunot!" And so it is always, if you exclaim, "Oh, the spirit of the men of France!" and a Frenchman's ears catch your words, he will correct, "Ah, but the women!"

And the women do stand above all other women, they have had such opportunity for heroism. Whose heart does not beat the faster when the names Soisson and Mme. Macherez are spoken! The mayor and the council gone, she assumes the office and keeps order while German shells fall thick on the town. And then the enemy enters, and asks for the mayor, and she replies, "Le maire, c'est moi." And then do we women not like to think of Mlle. Deletete staying at her post in the telegraph office in Houplines in spite of German bombardments, and calmly facing tormentors, when they smashed her instruments and threatened her with death. One-tenth of France in the enemy's hands, and in each village and town some woman staying behind to nurse the sick and wounded, to calm the population when panic threatens, to stand invincible between the people and their conquerors!

It is very splendid!--the French man holding steady at the front, the French woman an unyielding second line of defense. But what of France? Words of praise must not swallow our sense of obligation. Let us with our hundred millions of people face the figures. The death rate in France, not counting the military loss, is twenty per thousand, with a birth rate of eight per thousand. In Paris for the year ending August, 1914, there were forty-eight thousand nine hundred and seventeen births; in the year ending in the same month, 1916, the births dropped to twenty-six thousand one hundred and seventy-nine. The total deaths for that year in all France were one million, one hundred thousand, and the births three hundred and twelve thousand.

France is profoundly, infinitely sad. She has cause. I shall never forget looking into the very depths of her sorrow when I was at Creil. A great drive was in progress, the wounded were being brought down from the front, troops hurried forward. Four different regiments passed as I sat at déjeuner. The restaurant, full of its noonday patrons, was a typical French café giving on the street. We could have reached out and touched the soldiers. They marched without music, without song or word, marched in silence. Some of the men were from this very town; their little sons, with set faces, too, walked beside them and had brought them bunches of flowers. The people in the restaurant never spoke above a whisper, and when the troops passed were as silent as death. There was no cheer, but just a long, wistful gaze, the soldiers looking into their eyes, they into the soldiers'.

But France can bear her burden, can solve her problem if we lift our full share from her bent shoulders. Her women can save the children if the older men, relieved by our young soldiers, come back from the trenches, setting women free for the work of child saving. France can rebuild her villages if her supreme architects, her skilled workers are replaced in the trenches by our armies. France can renew her spirit and save her body if her experts in science, if her poets and artists are sent back to her, and our less great bare their breasts to the Huns.

V
MOBILIZING WOMEN IN GERMANY

The military mobilization of Germany was no more immediate and effective than the call to arms for women. On August 1, 1914, the summons went out, and German women were at once part of the smooth running machine of efficiency.

The world says the Kaiser has been preparing for war for forty years. The world means that he has been preparing the fighting force. The sword and guns were to be ready. But the military arm of the nation, the German government believes, is but the first line of attack; the people are the second line, and so they, too, in all their life activities, were not forgotten. The military aristocracy has never neglected the function of women in the state. The definition of their function may differ from ours, but that there is a function is recognized, and it is related to the other vital social organs.

Slowly, through the last half of the nineteenth century, there had grown up clubs among German women focusing on a definite bit of work, or crystallizing about an idea. Germany even had suffrage societies. Politics, however, were forbidden by the government; women were not allowed to hang on the fringe of a meeting held to discuss men's politics. But the women of the Fatherland were free to pool their ideas in philanthropic and hygienic corners, and venture out at times on educational highways. The Froebel societies had many a contest with the government, for to the military mind, the gentle pedagogue's theories seemed subversive of discipline as enforced by spurs and bayonets.

These clubs, covering every trade and profession, every duty and every aspiration of women, were dotted over the German Empire. At last they drew together in a federation. The government looked on. It saw a machine created, and believing in thorough organization, no doubt gave thought to the possibilities of the Bund deutscher, Frauenvereine. At the outbreak of war, Dr. Gertrud Baumer was president of the Bund. She was a leader of great ability, marshalling half a million of women. No other organization was so widespread and well-knit, except perhaps Der Vaterlandische Frauenverein with its two thousand one hundred and fifty branches. It was evangelical and military. The Empress was its patron. Its popular name is the "Armée der Kaiserin."

There the two great national societies stood--one aristocratic, the other democratic, one appealing to the ruling class, the other holding in bonds of fellowship the rich and the poor, the urban and the rural, the professional and the industrial woman.

Every belligerent president or premier has faced exactly the same perplexity. What woman, what society, is to be recognized as leader? The question has brought beads of perspiration to the foreheads of statesmen.

France solved the difficulty urbanely. It said "yes" to each and all. It promised coöperation and kept the promise. By affably--always affably and hospitably--accepting this service from one society, and suggesting another pressing need to its competitor, it sorted out capabilities, and warded off duplication. Perhaps this did not bring the fullest efficiency, but the loss was more than made up, no doubt, by a free field for initiative. Britain ignored all existing organizations of women, and after a year and a half of puzzlement created a separate government department for their mobilization. America struck out still another course. It took the heads of several national societies, bound them in one committee, to which it gave, perhaps with the idea of avoiding any danger of friction, neither power nor funds.

Germany faced the same critical moment for decision. The government wanted efficient use of woman-power on the land, in the factory, in the home, and that quickly. It made use of the best existing machinery. Dr. Gertrud Baumer visited the Ministerium des Innern, and on August 1 she issued a call for the mobilization of women for service to the Fatherland in the Nationale Frauendienst. Under the aegis of the government, with the national treasury behind her, Dr. Baumer summoned the women of the Empire. By order, every woman and every organization of women was to fall in line under the Frauendienst in each village and city for "the duration of the war."[3]

In each army district, the government appointed a woman as directress, and by order to town and provincial authorities made the Frauendienst part of local executive affairs.

Among the immediate duties laid upon the Frauendienst by the authorities was the task of registering all needy persons, of providing cheap eating places, opening workrooms, and setting up nurseries for children, especially for those who were motherless and those whose fathers had fallen at the front and whose mothers were in some gainful pursuit. With these duties went the administrative service of coöperating with the government in "keeping up an even supply of foodstuffs, and controlling the buying and selling of food."

Germany anticipated as did no other belligerent the unemployment which would follow a declaration of war, and prepared to meet the condition. A great deal of army work, such as tent sewing, belts for cartridges, bread sacks, and sheets for hospitals, was made immediately available for the women thrown out of luxury trades. In the first month of the war the Frauendienst opened work-rooms in all great centers; machinery was installed by magic and through the six work-rooms in Berlin alone twenty-three thousand women were given paid employment in one week.

Such efforts could not, of course, absorb the surplus labor, for unemployment was very great. Eighty percent of the women's hat-makers and milliners were out of work, seventy-two percent of the workers in glass and fifty-eight percent in china. The Frauendienst investigated two hundred and fifty-five thousand needy cases, and in Berlin alone found sixty thousand women who had lost their employment. Charity had to render help. Here, again, it is an example of the alertness of the organization and its close connection with the government that the Berlin magistracy deputed to twenty-three Hilfscommissionen from the Frauendienst the work of giving advice and charity relief to the unemployed. Knitting rooms were opened, clothing depots, mending rooms, where donated clothing was repaired, and in one month fifty-six thousand orders for milk, five hundred thousand for bread, and three hundred thousand for meals were distributed for the city authorities.

The adjustment to war requirements went on more quickly in Germany than in any other country. Before a year had passed the surplus hands had been absorbed, and a shortage of labor power was beginning to be felt.

And now opens the war drama set with the same scene everywhere. Women hurry forward to take up the burden laid down by men, and to assume the new occupations made necessary by the organization of the world for military conflict. To tell of Germany is merely to speak in bigger numbers. Women in munitions? Of course, well over the million mark. Trolley conductors? Of course, six hundred in Berlin alone before the first Christmas. Women are making the fuses, fashioning the big shells, and at the same heavy machines used by the men. That speaks volumes--the same heavy machines. Great Britain and France have in every case introduced lighter machinery for their women. But, whatever the conditions, in Germany the women are handling high explosives, sewing heavy saddlery, operating the heaviest drill machines. Women have been put on the "hardest jobs hitherto filled by men." In the German-Luxemburg Mining and Furnace Company at Differdingen, they are found doing work at the slag and blast furnaces which had always required men of great endurance. They work on the same shifts as the men, receive the same pay, but are not worked overtime "because they must go home and perform their domestic duties."

One feels the weight of the German system. Patient women shoulder double burdens. They always did.

In the Post and Telegraph department there is an army of fifty thousand women. The telephone service is entirely in their hands, and running more smoothly than formerly. Dr. Käthe Schirmacher declares comfortingly in the *Kriegsfrau* that "one must not forget that these women know many important bits of information--and keep silent." Women have learned to keep a secret!

One hundred and eighty nurses, experts with the X-ray, were in the front line dressing stations in the early days of the war, and before a week of conflict had passed women were in the Field Post, and Frau Reimer, organizer of official chauffeurs, was on the western line of attack.

Agriculture claims more women than any occupation in Germany. They were always on the farm, perhaps they are happier there now since they themselves are in command. It is said that "the peasants work in the boots and trousers of their husbands and ride in the saddle." War has liberated German women from the collar and put them on horseback!

But strangest and most unexpected of all is the professional and administrative use of women. The government has sent women architects and interior decorators to East Prussia to plan and carry through reconstruction work. Over a hundred--to be exact, one hundred and sixteen at last accounts--have taken the places of men in administrative departments connected with the railways. Many widows who have shown capacity have been put in government positions of importance formerly held by their husbands. Women have become farm managers, superintendents of dairy industries, and representatives of landed proprietors.

The disseminating of all instruction and information for women on war economies was delegated to the League of Women's Domestic Science Clubs. The Berlin course was held in no less a place than the Abgeordnetenhaus, and the Herrenhaus opened its doors wide on Rural Women's Day when Agricultural Week was held at the capital.

When the full history of the war comes to be written, no doubt one reason for Germany's marvelous power to stand so long against the world will be found in her use of every brain and muscle of the nation. This has been for her no exclusive war. Her entire people to their last ounce of energy have been engaged.

And this supreme service on the part of German women seeks democratic expression. From them comes the clearest, bravest word that has reached us across the border. The most hopeful sign is this manifesto from the suffrage organizations to the government: "Up to the present Germany has stood in the lowest rank of nations as regards women's rights. In most civilized lands women already have been given a large share in public affairs. German women have been granted nothing except within the most insignificant limits. In New Zealand, Australia and most American States, and even before the war in Finland and Norway, they had been given political rights; to-day, Sweden, Russia and many other countries give them a full or limited franchise. The war has brought a full victory to the women of England, Canada, Russia and Denmark, and large concessions are within sight in France, Holland and Hungary.

"Among us Germans not only the national but even the commercial franchise is denied, and even a share in the industrial and commercial courts. In the demand for the democratization of German public life our legislators do not seem even to admit the existence of women.

"But during the war the cooperation of women in public life has unostentatiously grown from year to year until to-day the number of women engaged in various callings in Germany exceeds the number of men.

"The work they are doing includes all spheres of male activity; without them it would no longer be possible to support the economic life of the people. Women have done their full share in the work of the community.

"Does not this performance of duty involve the right to share in the building up and extension of the social order?

"The women protest against this lack of political rights, in virtue both of their work for the community and of their work as human beings. They demand political equality with men. They demand the direct, equal and secret franchise for all legislative bodies, full equality in the communes and in legal representation of their interests.

"This first joint pronouncement on women's demands will be followed by others until the victory of our cause is won."

[3] "Die Frauenvereine jeder Stadt verbinden sich für die Dauer des Krieges zur Organization Nationaler Frauendienst die zu Berlin am 1ten August begründet wurde."

VI
WOMEN OVER THE TOP IN AMERICA

American women have begun to go over the top. They are going up the scaling-ladder and out into All Man's Land. Perhaps love of adventure tempts them, perhaps love of money, or a fine spirit of service, but whatever the propelling motive, we are seeing them make the venture.

There is nothing new in our day in a woman's being paid for her work--some of it. But she has never before been seen in America employed, for instance, as a section hand on a railway. The gangs are few and small as yet, but there the women are big and strong specimens of foreign birth. They "trim" the ballast and wield the heavy "tamping" tool with zest. They certainly have muscles, and are tempted to use them vigorously at three dollars a day.

In the machine shops where more skill than strength is called for, the American element with its quick wits and deft fingers predominates. Young women are working at the lathe with so much precision and accuracy that solicitude as to what would become of the world if all its men marched off to war is in a measure assuaged. In the push and drive of the industrial world, women are handling dangerous chemicals in making flash lights, and T.N.T. for high explosive shells. The American college girl is not as yet transmuting her prowess of the athletic field into work on the anvil, as is the university woman in England, but she has demonstrated her manual strength and skill on the farm with plough and harrow.

Women and girls answer our call for messenger service, and their intelligence and courtesy are an improvement upon the manners of the young barbarians of the race. Women operate elevators, lifting us with safety to the seventh heaven, or plunging us with precision to the depths. There were those at first who refused to entrust their lives to such frail hands, and there are still some who look concerned when they see a woman at the lever; but on the whole the elevator "girl" has gained the confidence of her public, and has gained it by skill, not by feminine wiles, for even men won't shoot into space with a woman at the helm whose sole equipment is charm. With need of less skill than the elevator operator, but more patience and tact in managing human nature, the woman conductor is getting her patrons into line. We are still a little embarrassed in her presence. We try not to stare at the well-set-up woman in her sensible uniform, while she on her part tries to look unconscious, and with much dignity accomplishes the common aim much more successfully than do we. She is so attentive to her duties, so courteous, and, withal, so calm and serious that I hope she will abide with us longer than the "duration of the war."

In short, America is witnessing the beginning of a great industrial and social change, and even those who regard the situation as temporary cannot doubt that the experience will have important reactions. The development is more advanced than it was in Great Britain at a corresponding time, for even before the United States entered the conflict women were being recruited in war industries. They have opened up every line of service. There is not an occupation in which a woman is not found.

When men go a-warring, women go to work.

A distinguished general at the end of the Cuban War, enlarging upon the poet's idea of woman's weeping rôle in wartime, said in a public speech: "When the country called, women put guns in the hands of their soldier boys and bravely sent them away. After the good-byes were said there was nothing for these women to do but to go back and wait, wait, wait. The excitement of battle was not for them. It was simply a season of anxiety and heartrending inactivity." Now the fact is, when a great call to arms is sounded for the men of a nation, women enlist in the industrial army. If women did indeed sit at home and weep, the enemy would soon conquer.

The dull census tells the thrilling story. Before our Civil War women were found in less than a hundred trades, at its close in over four hundred. The census of 1860 gives two hundred and eighty-five thousand women in gainful pursuits; that of 1870, one million, eight hundred and thirty-six thousand. Of the Transvaal at war, this story was told to me by an English officer. He led a small band of soldiers down into the Boer country, on the north from Rhodesia, as far as he dared. He "did not see a man," even boys as young as fifteen had joined the army. But at the post of economic duty stood the Boer woman; she was tending the herds and carrying on all the work of the farm. She was the base of supplies. That was why the British finally put her in a concentration camp. Her man could not be beaten with her at his back.

War compels women to work. That is one of its merits. Women are forced to use body and mind, they are not, cannot be idlers. Perhaps that is the reason military nations hold sway so long; their reign continues, not because they draw strength from the conquered nation, but because their women are roused to exertion. Active mothers ensure a virile race.

The peaceful nation, if its women fall victims to the luxury which rapidly increasing wealth brings, will decay. If there come no spiritual awakening, no sense of responsibility of service, then perhaps war alone can save it. The routing of idleness and ease by compulsory labor is the good counterbalancing some of the evil.

The rapidly increasing employment of women to-day, then, is the usual, and happy, accompaniment of war. But the development has its opponents, and that is nothing new, either. Let us look them over one by one. The most mischievous objector is the person, oftenest a woman, who says the war will be short, and fundamental changes, therefore, should not be made. This agreeable prophecy does not spring from a heartening belief in victory, but only from the procrastinating attitude, "Why get ready?" To prepare for anything less certain than death seems folly to many of the sex, over-trained in patient waiting.

Then there is the official who constantly sees the seamy side of industrial life and who concludes--we can scarcely blame him--that "it would be well if women were excluded entirely from factory life." The bad condition of industrial surroundings bulks large in his mind, and the value of organized work to us mortals bulks small. We are all too inclined to forget that the need for work cannot be eliminated, but the unhealthy process in a dangerous trade can. Clean up the factory, rather than clean out the women, is a sound slogan.

And then comes the objector who is exercised as to the effect of paid work upon woman's charm. Solicitude on this score is often buried in a woman's heart. It was a woman, the owner of a large estate, who when proposing to employ women asked how many men she would have to hire in addition, "to dig, plough and do all the hard work." On learning that the college units do everything on a farm, she queried anxiously, "But how about their corsets?" To the explanation, "They don't wear any," came the regret, "What a pity to make themselves so unattractive!"

I have heard fear expressed, too, lest sex attraction be lost through work on army hats, the machinery being noisy and the operative, if she talk, running the danger of acquiring a sharp, high voice. One could but wonder if most American women work on army hats.

Among the women actually employed, I have found without exception a fine spirit of service. So many of them have a friend or brother "over there," that backing up the boys makes a strong personal appeal. But some of the women who have left factory life behind are adopting an attitude towards the present industrial situation as lacking in vision as in patriotism. Throughout a long discussion in which some of these women participated I was able to follow and get their point of view. To them a woman acting as a messenger, an elevator operator, or a trolley conductor, was anathema, and the tempting of women into these employments seemed but the latest vicious trick of the capitalist. The conductor in her becoming uniform was most reprehensible, and her evident satisfaction in her job suggested to her critics that she merely was trying to play a melodramatic part "as a war hero." In any case, the conductor's occupation was one no woman should be in, "crowded and pushed about as she is." It was puzzling to know why it was regarded as right for a woman to pay five cents and be pushed, and unbecoming for another woman to be paid eighteen dollars and ninety cents a week and run the risk of a jolt when stepping outside her barrier.

But the ideals of yesterday fail to make their appeal. It is not the psychological moment to urge, on the ground of comfort, the woman's right to protection. The contrast between the trenches and the street car or factory is too striking. But it is, however, the exact moment to plead for better care of workers, both women and men, because their health and skill are as necessary in attaining the national aim as the soldiers' prowess and well-being. It is the time to advocate the protection of the worker from long hours, because the experience of Europe has proved that a greater and better output is achieved when a short day is strictly adhered to, when the weekly half-holiday is enjoyed, and Sunday rest respected. The United States is behind other great industrial countries in legal protection for the workers. War requirements may force us to see in the health of the worker the greatest of national assets. Meantime, whether approved or not, the American woman is going over the top. Four hundred and more are busy on aeroplanes at the Curtiss works. The manager of a munition shop where to-day but fifty women are employed, is putting up a dormitory to accommodate five hundred. An index of expectation! Five thousand are employed by the Remington Arms Company at Bridgeport. At the International Arms and Fuse Company at Bloomfield, New Jersey, two thousand, eight hundred are employed. The day I visited the place, in one of the largest shops women had only just been put on the work, but it was expected that in less than a month they would be found handling all of the twelve hundred machines under that one roof alone.

The skill of the women staggers one. After a week or two they master the operations on the "turret," gauging and routing machines. The best worker on the "facing" machine is a woman. She is a piece worker, as many of the women are, and is paid at the same rate as men. This woman earned, the day I saw her, five dollars and forty cents. She tossed about the fuse parts, and played with that machine, as I would with a baby. Perhaps it was in somewhat the same spirit--she seemed to love her toy.

Most of the testers and inspectors are women. They measure the parts step by step, and weigh the completed fuse, carrying off the palm for reliability. The manager put it, "for inspection the women are more conscientious than men. They don't measure or weigh just one piece, shoving along a half-dozen untouched and let it go at that. They test each." That did not surprise me, but I was not prepared to hear that the women do not have so many accidents as men, or break the machines so often. In explanation, the manager threw over an imaginary lever with vigor sufficient to shake the factory, "Men put their whole strength on, women are more gentle and patient."

Nor are the railways neglecting to fill up gaps in their working force with women. The Pennsylvania road, it is said, has recruited some seven hundred of them. In the Erie Railroad women are not only engaged as "work classifiers" in the locomotive clerical department, but hardy Polish women are employed in the car repair shops. They move great wheels as if possessed of the strength of Hercules. And in the locomotive shops I found women working on drill-press machines with ease and skill. Just as I came up to one operator, she lifted an engine truck-box to the table and started drilling out the studs. She had been at the work only a month, and explained her skill by the information that she was Swedish, and had always worked with her husband in their auto-repair shop. All the other drill-press hands and the "shapers," too, were Americans whose husbands, old employees, were now "over there." Not one seemed to have any sense of the unusual; even the little blond check-clerk seated in her booth at the gates of the works with her brass discs about her had in a few months' time changed a revolution into an established custom. She and the discs seemed old friends. Women are adaptable.

Copyright by Underwood and Underwood
The daily round in the Erie Railroad workshops.

But everywhere I gathered the impression that the men are a bit uneasy. A foreman in one factory pointed out a man who "would not have voted for suffrage" had he guessed that women were "to rush in and gobble everything up." I tried to make him see that it wasn't the vote that gave the voracious appetite, but necessity or desire to serve. And in any case, women do not push men out, they push them up. In not a single instance did I hear of a man being turned off to make a place for a woman. He had left his job to go into the army, or was advanced to heavier or more skilled work.

As to how many women have supplanted men, or poured into the new war industries, no figures are available. One guess has put it at a million. But that is merely a guess. I have seen them by the tens, the hundreds, the thousands. The number is large and rapidly increasing. We may know that something important is happening when even the government takes note. The United States Labor Department has recognized the new-comers by establishing a Division of Women's Work with branches in every State. It looks as if these bureaus of employment would not be idle, with a showing of one thousand, five hundred applicants the first week the New York office was opened. It is to be hoped that this government effort will save the round pegs from getting into the square holes.

But even the round peg in the round hole brings difficulties. When Adam Smith asserted that of all sorts of luggage man was the most difficult to move, he forgot woman! The instant women are carried into a new industry, they bring with them puzzling problems. Where shall we put their coats and picture hats, how shall we cover up their hair, what shall we feed them with? They must have lockers and rest rooms, caps and overalls, and above all, canteens. The munition workers, the conductors, in fact, all women in active work, get prodigiously hungry. They have made a regiment of dietitians think about calories. Here is what one of the street railways in New York City offered them on a given day:--

Tomato soup 10c. or with an order 5c.
Roast leg of veal 16c.
Beef 16c.
Lamb fricassee 16c.
Ham steak 16c.
Liver and onions 16c.
Sirloin steak 30c.
Small steak 20c.
Ham and eggs 20c.
Ham omelet 20c.
Regular dinner Soup, meat,
  Vegetable,
  Dessert, coffee   25c.
Rice pudding 5c.
Pie 5c.
Cake 5c.
Banana or orange 5c.

The canteen is open every hour of the twenty-four, and the women conductors at the end of each run usually take a bite, and then have a substantial meal during the long break of an hour and a half in the middle of the ten-hour day.

Another problem brought to us by women in industry is, how can we house them? The war industries have drawn large numbers to new centers. The haphazard accommodation which men win put up with, won't satisfy women. They demand more, and get more. To attract the best type of women the munition plants are putting up dormitories to accommodate hundreds of workers, and are making their plants more attractive, with rest rooms and hospital accommodation. Take, for instance, the Briggs and Stratton Company, which in order to draw high grade workers built its new factory in one of the best sections of Milwaukee. The workrooms are as clean as the proverbial Dutch woman's doorstep. From the top of the benches to the ceiling the walls are glass to ensure daylight in every corner, and by night the system of indirect lighting gives such perfectly diffused light that not a heavy shadow falls anywhere. And the hospital room and nurse--well, one would rejoice to have an accident daily!

The factory may become the exemplar for the home. The professional woman is going over the top, and with a good opinion of herself. "I can do this work better than any man," was the announcement made by a young woman from the Pacific Coast as she descended upon the city hall in an eastern town, credentials in her hand, and asked for the position of city chemist. There was not a microbe she did not know to its undoing, or a deadly poison she could not bring from its hiding place. The town had suffered from graft, and the mayor, thinking a woman might scare the thieves as well as the bacteria, appointed the chemist who believed in herself. And she is just one of many who have been taking up such work.

Formerly two-thirds of the positions filled by the New York Intercollegiate Bureau of Occupations were secretarial or teaching positions; now three-fourths of its applicants have been placed as physicists, chemists, office managers, sanitary experts, exhibit secretaries, and the like. The temporary positions used to outnumber the permanent placements; at present the reverse is true. Of the women placed, four times as many as formerly get salaries ranging above eighteen hundred dollars a year.

The story told at the employment bureaus in connection with professional societies and clubs such as the Chemists' Club is the same. Women are being placed not merely as teachers of chemistry or as routine laboratory workers in hospitals, but also as experimental and control chemists in industrial plants. In the great rolling mills they are testing steel, at the copper smelters they are found in the laboratories. The government has thrown doors wide open to college-trained women. They are physicists and chemists in the United States Bureaus of Standards, Mines, and Soils, sanitary experts in military camps, research chemists in animal nutrition and fertilizers at state experiment stations.

But the industrial barrier is the one most recently scaled. Women are now found as analytical, research or control chemists in the canneries, in dye and electrical works, in flour and paper mills, in insecticide companies, and cement works. They test the steel that will carry us safely on our journeys, they pass upon the chemical composition of the flavor in our cake, as heads of departments in metal refining companies they determine the kind of copper battery we shall use, and they have a finger in our liquid glues, household oils and polishes.

And the awakened spirit of social responsibility has opened new callings. The college woman not only is beginning to fill welfare positions inside the factory, but is acting as protective officer in towns near military camps. Perhaps one of the newest and most interesting positions is that of "employment secretary." The losing of employees has become so serious and general that big industries have engaged women who devote their time to looking up absentees and finding out why each worker left.

And so we see on all hands women breaking through the old accustomed bounds.

Not only as workers but as voters, the war has called women over the top. Since that fateful August, 1914, four provinces of Canada and the Dominion itself have raised the banner of votes for women. Nevada and Montana declared for suffrage before the war was four months old, and Denmark enfranchised its women before the year was out. And when America went forth to fight for democracy abroad, Arkansas, Michigan, Vermont, Nebraska, North Dakota, Rhode Island, began to lay the foundations of freedom at home, and New York in no faltering voice proclaimed full liberty for all its people. Lastly Great Britain has enfranchised its women, and surely the Congress of the United States will not lag behind the Mother of Parliaments!

The world is facing changes as great as the breaking up of the feudal system. Causes as fundamental, more wide-spread, and more cataclysmic are at work than at the end of the Middle Ages. Among the changes none is more marked than the intensified development in what one may call, for lack of a better term, the woman movement. The advance in political freedom has moved steadily forward during the past quarter of a century, but in the last three years progress has been intense and striking.

The peculiarity in attainment of political democracy for women has lain in the fact that while for men economic freedom invariably preceded political enfranchisement, in the case of women the conferring of the vote in no single case was related to the stage which the enfranchised group had attained in the matter of economic independence. Nowhere were even those women who were entirely lacking in economic freedom, excluded on that account from any extension of suffrage. Even in discussions of the right of suffrage no reference has ever been made, in dealing with women's claim, to the relation, universally recognized in the case of men, of political enfranchisement to economic status. Serfdom gave way to the wage system before democracy developed for men, and the colored man was emancipated before he was enfranchised. For this reason the coming of women as paid workers over the top may be regarded as epoch-making.

In any case, self-determination is certainly a strong element in attaining any real political freedom.

Complete service to their country in this crisis may lead women to that economic freedom which will change a political possession into a political power. But the requirement is readiness to do, and to do well, the task which offers. Man-power must give itself unreservedly at the front. Women must show not only eagerness but fitness to substitute for man-power. It will hearten the nation, help to make the path clear, if individual women declare that though the call to them has not yet come for a definite service, the time of waiting will not be spent in complaint, nor yet in foolish busy-ness, but in careful and conscientious training for useful work.

Each woman must prepare so that when the nation's need arises, she can stand at salute and say, "Here is your servant, trained and ready." Women are not driven over the top. Through self-discipline, they go over it of their own accord.

VII
EVE'S PAY ENVELOPE

No woman is a cross between an angel and a goose. She is a very human creature. She has many of man's sins and some virtues of her own.

Moving up from slavery through all the various forms of serfdom--attachment to the soil, confinement to a given trade, exclusion from citizenship, payment in kind, on to full economic freedom, men have shown definite reactions at each step. Women respond to the same stimuli.

The free man is a better worker than slave or serf. So is the free woman. All the old gibes at her ineptitudes have broken their points against the actualities of her ability as a wage worker. The free man is more alert to obligation, more conscientious in performance, than the bond servant. So is the free woman. With pay envelope, or pension, Eve is a better helpmate and mother than ever before.

The free man carries a lighter heart than the villain. So does the free woman. Men have always borne personal grief more easily than women; observers remarked the fact. The reason is the same. An absorbing occupation, ordered and regarded as important, which brings a return allowing the recipient to patronize what he or she thinks wise, that brings happiness, not boisterous, but dignified. It may be a holocaust through which Eve gains that pay envelope, but the material possession brings gratification nevertheless. It is a tiny straw showing the set of the wind that leisure class British women, however large their unearned bank account, show no reluctance to accept pay for their work, and full responsibility in their new position of employee.

Women are supposed to have liked to serve for mere love of service, for love of child, love of husband. There is, of course, many a subtle relation which can't be weighed and paid for; but toil, even for one's very own hearthstone, can be valued in hard cash. The daughters of Eve, no less than the sons of Adam, react happily to a recognition that expresses itself in a fair wage.

The verdict comes from all sides that women were never more content. Of course they are content. The weight of suppression is being lifted. For many their drudgery is for the first time paid for. Is not that invigorating? The pay envelope is equal to that of men. Is not that a new experience giving self-respect? Eve often finds her pay envelope heavier than that of the man working at her side. Right there in her hand, then, she holds proof that the old prejudice against her as an inferior worker is ill-founded.

Women are finding themselves. Even America's Eve discovers that pains and aches are not "woman's lot." She is under no curse in the twentieth century. With eighteen dollars a week for ringing up fares, and a possible thirty-five for "facing" fuse-parts, nothing can persuade her to be poor-spirited. She radiates the atmosphere, "I am needed!" Doors fly open to her. She is welcome everywhere. No one seems to be able to get too many of her kind. Politicians compete for her favor, employers quarrel over her. It makes her breathe deep to have the Secretary of the Navy summon her to the United States arsenals, pay her for her work, and call her a patriot.

In the well-lighted factory of the Briggs and Stratton Company, Milwaukee, the girls are comfortably and becomingly garbed for work.

And with the pay envelope women remain clearly human. Their purchases often reflect past denials, rather than present needs or even tastes. When set free one always buys what the days of dependence deprived one of. One of Boston's leading merchants told me that Selfridge in London was selling more jaunty ready-to-wear dresses than ever before. It was part of John Bull's discipline in ante-bellum dependent days to keep his women folk dowdy. The Lancashire lass with head shawl and pattens, the wearer of the universal sailor hat, in these days of independence and pounds, shillings and pence, are taking note of the shop windows. And John is not turning his eyes away from his women folk in their day of self-determination.

But it is not to be concluded that it is all beer and skittles for Eve. With a pay envelope and a vote come responsibilities. Public sympathy has backed up laws cutting down long hours of work for women. The trade unions, with a thought to possible competitors, have favored protecting them from night work. Has Eve been a bit spoiled? Has she let herself too easily be classed with children and allowed a line to be drawn between men and women in industry? Is it a bit of woman's proverbial logic to demand special protection, and at the same time insist upon "equal pay for equal work"?

The hopelessness of attaining the promise of the slogan is well illustrated in the case of a gray haired woman I once met in a London printing shop. In her early days she had been one of the women taken on by the famous printing firm of McCorquodale. That was before protective legislation applied to women. She became a highly skilled printer, earning more than any man in the shop. When there was pressure of work she was always one of the group of experts chosen to carry through the rush order. That meant on occasion overtime or night work. Then she went on to tell me how her skill was checked in her very prime. Regulations as to women's labor were gradually fixed in the law. All the printers in the shop, she said, favored the laws limiting her freedom but not theirs. Soon her wages reflected the contrast. Her employer called her to his office one day and explained, "I cannot afford to pay you as much as the men any longer. You are not worth as much to me, not being able to work Saturday afternoon, at night, or overtime." She was put on lower grade work and her pay envelope grew slight.

This woman was not discussing the value of shorter working hours, she was pointing out that "equal pay" cannot rule for an entire group of workers when restrictions apply to part of the group and not to the whole body. We meet here, not a theory, but an incontrovertible fact. Pay is not equal, and cannot be, where conditions are wholly unequal. Protection for the woman worker means exactly what it would mean for the alien man if by law he were forbidden to work Saturday afternoon, overtime or at night, while the citizen worker was without restriction. The alien would be cut off from advancement in every trade in which he did not by overwhelming numbers dominate the situation, he would be kept to lower grade processes, he would receive much lower pay than the unprotected worker.

What common sense would lead us to expect in the hypothetical case of an alien man, has happened for the woman worker. Oddly enough she has not herself asked for this protection, but it has been urged very largely by women not of the industrial class. Women teachers, doctors, lawyers, women of leisure are the advocates of special legislation for industrial women. And yet in their own case they are entirely reasonable, and ask no favors. The woman teacher, and quite truly, insists that she works as hard and as long hours as the man in her grade of service, and on that sound foundation she builds her just demand for equal pay. Women doctors and lawyers have never asked for other than a square deal in their professions.

It would be well, perhaps, if industrial women were permitted to guide their own ship. They have knowledge enough to reach a safe harbor. There was a hint that they were about to assume the helm when the rank and file of union workers voted down at the conference of the Women's Trade Union League the resolution proposing a law to forbid women acting as conductors. It was also suggestive when a woman rose and asked of the speaker on dangerous trades, whether "men did not suffer from exposure to fumes, acids and dust."

Women have so long been urging that they are people, that they have forgotten, perchance, that men are people also. Men respond to rest and recreation as do human beings of the opposite sex. All workers need, and both sexes should have, protection. But if only one sex in industrial life can have bulwarks thrown up about it, men should be the favored ones just now. They are few, they are precious, they should be wrapped in cotton wool.

The industrial woman should stand unqualifiedly for the exclusion of children from gainful pursuits. Many years ago the British government had Miss Collett, one of the Labor Correspondents of the Board of Trade, make a special study of the influence of the employment of married women on infant mortality. The object was to prove that there was direct cause and effect. The investigator, after an exhaustive study covering many industrial centers, brought back the report, "Not proven." But the statistics showed one most interesting relation. In districts where the prevailing custom permitted the employment of children as early as the law allowed, infant mortality was high, and in districts where few children were employed, infant mortality was low. No explanation of this striking revelation was made in the report, but many who commented on the tables, pointed out that the wide-spread employment of the population in its early years sapped the vitality of the community to such an extent that its offspring were weakened. In other words, the employment of the immature child, more than the employment of that child when grown and married, works harm to the race.

The woman with a pay envelope must not, then, be willing to swell the family budget by turning her children into the wage market. For if she does, she creates a dangerous competitor for herself, and puts in certain jeopardy the virility of her nation. But in this war time women have secured more than new and larger pay envelopes, for each belligerent has reckoned up the woman's worth as mother in coin of the realm. It is enough to turn Eve's head--pay and pensions accorded her all at once.

Allowances to dependents are more, however, than financial expedients. They are part of the psychological stage-setting of the Great War. The fighting man must be more than well-fed, well-clothed, well-equipped, more than assured of care if ill or wounded; he must have his mind undisturbed by conditions at home. Governments now know that there must be no just cause for complaint in the family at the rear, if the man at the front is to be fully effective. In the interest of the fighting line, governments dare not leave the home to the haphazard care of charity.

And so the great belligerents have adopted systems for an uninterrupted flow of money aid to the hearthstone. The wife feels dependence on the nation for which she and her man are making sacrifices, the soldier has a sense of closer relationship with the country's cause for which he fights. Content at home and sense of gratitude in the trenches build up loyalty everywhere. The state allowance answers an economic want and a psychological necessity.

It is part of our national lack of technique that we were slow to make provision for the dependents of enlisted men, and even then were not whole hearted. It may have been our inherited distrust of the conscript that led us to feel that only by his volunteering something will a precious antidote be administered to the spirit of the drafted man. To protect his individualism from taint, the United States soldier must bear part of the financial burden. Europe, on the other hand, is working on a basis of reciprocity. The nation exacts service from the man and gives complete service to his dependents. In America the man is bound to serve the community, but the community is not bound to serve him. And yet in our case there is peculiar need of this even exchange of obligations. The care of parents in the United States falls directly upon their children, while some of our allies had, even before the war, carefully devised laws regulating pensions to the aged.

But first let us get the simple skeleton of the various allowance laws in mind. The scale of the allowance in different countries adapts itself to national standards and varying cost of living. The Canadian allowance seems the most generous. At least one-half of the soldier's pay is given directly to his dependents. The government gives an additional twenty dollars and the donations of the

Patriotic Fund bring up the monthly allowance of a wife with three children to sixty dollars. The allowance, as might be expected, is low in Italy. The soldier's wife gets eight-tenths of a lira a day, each child four-tenths lira, and either a father or mother alone eight-tenths lira, or if both are living, one and three-tenths lire together. The British allowance is much higher, the wife getting twelve shillings and sixpence a week. If she has one child, the weekly allowance rises to nineteen and sixpence; if two children, to twenty-four and sixpence; if three, to twenty-eight shillings; and if there are four or more children, the mother receives three shillings a week for each extra child.

Between the extremes of Italy and England stands France, the wife receiving one franc twenty-five centimes a day, each child under sixteen years of age twenty-five centimes, and a dependent parent seventy-five centimes. Japan grants no government allowance. A Japanese official, in response to my inquiry, wrote, "Relations the first and friends the next try to help the dependents as far as possible, but if they have neither relatives nor friends who have sufficient means to help them, then the association consisting of ladies or the municipal officials afford subvention to them."

Under the law passed by Congress in October, 1917, an American private receiving thirty-three dollars a month when on service abroad must allot fifteen dollars a month to his wife, and the government adds to this twenty-five dollars, and if there is one child, an additional ten dollars, with five dollars for each additional child. A man can secure an allowance from the government of ten dollars a month to a dependent parent, if he allots five dollars a month. Such are the bare bones of the allowance schemes of the Allies on the western front

In the United States the general policy of exemption boards, as suggested by the central authorities, is most disciplinary as regards women. Their capacity for self-support is rigidly inquired into. Our men are definitely urging women to a position of economic independence. The aim is, while securing soldiers for the army, to relieve the government of the expense of dependency on the part of women. There is no doubt that our men at least are faced toward the future. No less indicative is it of a new world that the allowance laws of all the western belligerents recognize common-law marriages. In our own law, marriage is "presumed if the man and woman have lived together in the openly acknowledged relation of husband and wife during two years immediately preceding the date of the declaration of war." And the illegitimate child stands equal with the legitimate provided the father acknowledges the child or has been "judicially ordered or decreed to contribute" to the child's support.

Men are feminists. Their hearts have softened even towards the wife's relatives, for the word "parent" is not only broad enough to cover the father, mother, grandparents or step-father and mother of the man, but "of the spouse" also. Thus passeth the curse of the mother-in-law.

One need not be endowed with the spirit of prophecy to foretell that "allowances" in war time will broaden out into motherhood pensions in peace times. It would be an ordinary human reaction should the woman enjoying a pension refuse to give up, on the day peace is declared, her quickly acquired habit of holding the purse strings. That would be accepting international calm at the expense of domestic differences. The social value of encouraging the mother's natural feeling of responsibility toward her child by putting into her hands a state pension is being, let us note, widely tested, and may demonstrate the wisdom and economy of devoting public funds to mothers rather than to crêches and juvenile asylums.

The allowance laws may prove the charter of woman's liberties; her pay envelope may become her contract securing the right of self-determination.

VIII
POOLING BRAINS

"Employ them." This was the advice given to a large conference of women met to discuss business opportunities for their sex. The advice was vouchsafed by a young lawyer after the problem of opening wider fields to women in the legal profession had been looked at from every angle, only to end in the question, "What can we do to increase their practice?" She spoke with animation, as if she had found the key to the situation, "Employ them." Perhaps more self-accusation than determination to mend their ways was roused by the short and pointed remark.

The advice has wider application. Taking thirty names of women at random, I learned in response to an inquiry that only four had women physicians, two had women lawyers, and only one, a woman dentist. Twenty-five women of large real estate holdings had never even for the most unimportant work secured the services of an architect of their own sex. Further inquiry brought out the fact that of a long list of women's clubs and associations which have built or altered property for their purposes, only one had engaged a woman architect.

Perhaps it is indicative of a lack of nothing more serious than a sense of humor, that we women unite and, apparently without embarrassment, demand that masculine presidents, governors, mayors and legislatures shall appoint women to office. This unabashed faith in the good will of men seems not misplaced, for not only do public men show some confidence in the official capacity of women, but to my inquiry as to whom was due their opportunities to "get on," business women invariably replied, "To men."

However, the loyalty of women to women is increasing, and their solidarity on sound lines of service is a thing of steady growth. Thoughtful women, for instance, do not wish a woman put in a position of responsibility simply because she is a woman, but they are even more opposed to having a candidate of peculiar fitness overlooked merely because she is not a man. While the conscientious and poised women are not willing to urge any and every woman for a given office, they do tenaciously hold that there are positions which cry aloud for women and for which the right women should he found. In conquering a fair field, women will have to pool their brains even more effectively than they have in the past.

Our efforts at combination are a mere mushroom growth compared with the generations of training our big brothers have had in pooling brains. War and the chase gave them their first lessons in cooperation, nor has war been a bad teacher for women.

Just as the Crimean War and our Civil War put Florence Nightingale and Clara Barton and the trained nurse on the map, this war is bringing the medical woman to the fore. Women surgeons and doctors, unlike many other groups, offer themselves fully trained for service. They know they have something to give, and they know the soldiers' need.

According to an official statement, the emergency call of the army for men physicians and surgeons fell two thousand short of being answered. The necessity of the soldier and the skill of the women will no doubt in the end be brought effectively together; for although the government of the United States, like Great Britain in the early days of the war, has left to ever farseeing France the honor of extending hospitality to American women doctors, their strong national organization, with a membership of four thousand, will in time, no doubt, persuade Uncle Sam to take his plucky women doctors over the top under the Stars and Stripes! Organization crystallized about an unselfish desire and skilled ability to serve is irresistible.

The pooling of the brains of women that has been going on on a country-wide scale for more than a half-century bears analyzing. These associations have almost invariably centered about a service to be rendered. Even the first petition for political enfranchisement urged it as the "duty of the women of this country to secure to themselves the elective franchise." Unselfishness draws numbers as a magnet draws steel filings. The spirit of service lying at the heart of the great national organizations made possible quick response to new duties immediately upon our entrance into the war. The suffragists said, We wish to serve and we are ready for service. The government used their wide-spread net of local centers for purposes of registrations and war appeals.

Naturally there were many efforts more foolish than effective in the universal rush to help. America was not peculiar in this, nor for the matter of that, were women. War!--it does make the blood course through the veins. Every generous citizen cries aloud, "What can I do?" Perhaps men are a little more voluble than women, their emotions not finding such immediate and approved vent along clicking needles and tangled skeins of wool. On the whole, the initiative and organizing ability of women has stood out supremely.

Of the two departments of the Red Cross which are still left in the command of women, the Bureau of Nursing, with Miss Delano at its head, mobilized immediately three thousand of the fourteen thousand nurses enrolled. The first Red Cross Medical Unit with its full quota of sixty-five nurses completely equipped stood on European soil before an American soldier was there. Of the forty-nine units ready for service, twelve, with from sixty-five to one hundred nurses each, are now in France. Two of the five units organized for the navy, each with its forty active nurses and twenty reserves, are established abroad, and two hundred and thirty nurses are already in active naval service here. Miss Delano holds constantly in reserve fifteen hundred nurses as emergency detachments, a reservoir from which some eight hundred have been drawn for cantonment hospitals. An inflow of nearly one thousand nurses each month keeps the reservoir ready to meet the drain.

The Chapter work-rooms sprang up at a call in the night. No one can help admiring their well-ordered functioning. There may be criticism, grumbling, but the work-room is moving irresistibly, like a well-oiled machine. And women are the motive power from start to finish. The Chapters, with their five million members joined in three thousand units over the United States, are so many monuments to the ability of women for detail. Once mobilized, the women have thus far been able to serve two thousand war hospitals with surgical dressings, and to send abroad thirteen million separate articles packed carefully, boxed, labelled and accounted for on their books.

Not only does this directing of manual work stand to the credit of the Chapters, but they have given courses of lectures in home nursing and dietetics to thirty-four thousand women, and in first aid; ten thousand classes have been held and seventy-five thousand certificates issued to the proficient. Certainly one object of the Red Cross, "to stimulate the volunteer work of women," has been accomplished.

It is difficult to understand why, with such examples of women's efficiency before it, the Red Cross, founded by Clara Barton, places merely two bureaus in the hands of a woman, has chosen no woman as an officer, has put but one woman on its central and executive committee, and not a single woman on its present controlling body, the War Council. It may be that the protest against the centralization of all volunteer effort in the Red Cross, in spite of President Wilson's appeal, was due to the fact that women feared that their energies, running to other lines than nursing and surgical dressings, would be entirely sidetracked.

The honor of the splendid war work of the Young Women's Christian Association belongs to women. The War Work Council of the National Board of Young Women's Christian Associations shows an example of how immediately efficient an established organization can be in an emergency. As one sees its great War Fund roll up, one exclaims, "What money raisers women are!" The immediate demands upon the fund are for Hostess Houses at cantonments where soldiers can meet their women visitors, dormitories providing emergency housing for women employees at certain army centers, the strengthening of club work among the younger girls of the nation, profoundly affected by war conditions, and the sending of experienced organizers to coöperate with the women leaders of France and Russia and to install nurses' huts at the base hospitals of France. It makes one's heart beat high to think of women spending millions splendidly, they who have always been told to save pennies frugally! Well, those hard days were times of training; women learned not to waste.

A very worthy pooling of brains, because springing up with no tradition behind it, was the National League for Woman's Service. In six months it drew to itself two hundred thousand members and built organizations in thirty-nine States, established classes to train women for the new work opening to them, opened recreation centers and canteens at which were entertained on a single Sunday, at one center, eighteen hundred soldiers and sailors. So excellent was its Bureau of Registration and Information for women workers that the United States Department of Labor took over not only the files and methods of the Woman's League for Service, but the entire staff with Miss Obenauer at its head. If imitation is the sincerest flattery, what shall we say of complete adoption of work and workers, with an honorable "by your leave" and outspoken praise! And nothing could show a finer spirit of service than this yielding up of work initiated by a civil society and the willing passing of it into government hands.

Not only the Labor Department has established a special women's division with a woman at its head, but the Ordnance Office of the War Department has opened in its Industrial Service Section a woman's division, putting Miss Mary Van Kleeck in charge.

But still our government lags behind our Allies in mobilizing woman's power of initiative and her organizing faculty. The Woman's Committee of the Council of National Defense, appointed soon after the outbreak of war, still has no administrative power. As one member of the Committee says, "We are not allowed to do anything without the consent of the Council of National Defense. There is no appropriation for the Woman's Committee. We are furnished with headquarters, stationery, some printing and two stenographers, but nothing more. It is essential that we raise money to carry on the other expenses. The great trouble is that now, as always, men want women to do the work while they do the overseeing."

The women of the Motor Corps of the National League for Woman's Service refuting the traditions that women have neither strength nor endurance.

Perhaps holding the helm has become second nature to men simply because they have held the helm so long, but I am inclined to think they have a very definite desire to have women help steer the ship. Surely the readiness with which they are sharing their political power with women, would seem to indicate their wish for cooperation on a plan of perfect equality.

In any case, it is not necessary to hang on the skirts of government. America has always shown evidence of greater gift in private enterprise than state action. Perhaps women will demonstrate the national characteristic. It was farsightedness and enterprise that led the Intercollegiate Bureaus of Occupations, societies run for women by women, to strike out in this crisis and open up new callings for their clients, and still better, to persuade colleges and schools to modify curricula to meet the changed demands.

Women are often passed over because they are not prepared.

The Bureaus have found the demand for women in industrial chemistry and physics, for instance, to be greater than the supply because the graduates of women's colleges have not been carried far enough in mathematics, and in chemistry have been kept too much to theoretical text-book work. For example, the head of a certain industry was willing to give the position of chemist at his works to a woman. He needed some one to suggest changes in process from time to time, and to watch waste. He set down eight simple problems such as might arise any day in his factory for the candidates to answer. Some of the women, all college graduates, who had specialized in chemistry, could not answer a single problem, and none showed that grip of the science which would enable them to give other than rule of thumb solutions. He engaged a man.

In answering the questionnaire which the New York Bureau of Occupations sent to one hundred and twenty-five industrial plants, the manager in almost every case replied, in regard to the possibility of employing women in such positions as research or control chemists, that applicants were "badly prepared." As hand workers, too, women are handicapped by lack of knowledge of machinery. In this tool age, high school girls are cut off from technical education, although they are destined to carry on in large measure our skilled trades. I am told that in Germany many factories had to close because only women were available as managers, and they had not been fitted by business and technical schools for the task.

If women individually are looking for a soft place, if they are afraid, as one manager expressed it, "to put on overalls and go into a vat," even when their country is so in need of their service, it is futile for them to ask collectively for equal opportunity and equal pay; if they individually fail to prepare as for a life work, regarding themselves as but temporarily in business or a profession, their collective demand upon the world for a fair field and no favor will be as ineffective as illogical.

The doors stand wide open. It rests with women themselves as to whether they shall enter in.

To the steady appeals of the employment bureaus, backed by the stern facts of life, the colleges are yielding. On examination I found that curricula are already being modified. None but the sorriest pessimist could doubt the nature of the final outcome, on realizing the pooling of brains which is going on in such associations as the Intercollegiate Bureau of Occupations and the League for Business Opportunities. They work to the end of having young women not only soundly prepared for the new openings, but sensitive to the demands of a world set towards stern duty.

Not only is there call for a pooling of brains to look after the timid and unready, but there is need of combination to open the gates for the prepared and brave. Few who cheered the Red Cross nurses as they made their stirring march on Fifth Avenue, knew that those devoted women would, on entering the Military Nurse Corps, find themselves the only nurses among the Allies without a position of honor. The humiliation to our nurses in placing them below the orderlies in the hospitals is not only a blow to their esprit de corps, but a definite handicap to their efficiency. A nurse who was at the head of the nursing staff in a state hospital wrote from the front: "There is one thing the Nursing Committee needs to work for, and work hard, too, and that is, to make for nurses the rank of lieutenant. The Canadians have it, why not the Americans? You will find that it will make a tremendous difference. You see, there are no officers in our nursing personnel. One of our staff says we are the hired extras! It is really a great mistake." Uncle Sam may merely be waiting for a concentrated drive of public opinion against his tardy representatives.

Down the street they come, beginning their pilgrimage of alleviation and succor on the battlefields of France.

And why should it be necessary to urge that while scores of young men are dashing to death in endeavors to learn to fly, there are women unmobilized who know how to soar aloft in safety? They have never, it is true, been submitted to laboratory tests in twirlings and twistings, but they reach the zenith. Two carried off the records in long distance flights, but both have been refused admission to the Flying Corps. Will it need a campaign to secure for our army this efficient service? Must women pool their brains to have Ruth Law spread her protecting wings over our boys in France?

To any one who realizes the significance of the military situation as it stands, and who is cognizant of the contrast between Germany's use of her entire people in her national effort, and the slow mobilization of woman-power among the Allies and entire lack of anything worthy the name of mobilization of the labor-power of women in the United States, there will come a determination to bury every jealousy between woman and woman, all prejudice in men, to cut red tape in government, with the one object of combining all resources.

The full power of our men must be thrown into military effort. And, then, if as a nation we have brains to pool, we will not stand niggling, but will throw women doctors in to render their service, grant to the nurse corps what it needs to ensure efficiency, throw open the technical schools to girls as well as to boys, modify the college course to meet the facts of life. Each woman unprepared is a national handicap, each prejudice blocking the use of woman-power is treachery to our cause.

As to the final outcome of united thought and group action among women, no one can doubt. Contacts will rub off angles, capable service will break down sex prejudice and overcome government opposition. But there is not time to wait for the slow development of "final outcomes."

Women must pool their brains against their own shortcomings, and in favor of their own ability to back up their country now and here.

IX
"BUSINESS AS USUAL"

It is a platitude to say that America is the most extravagant nation on earth. The whole world tells us so, and we do not deny it, being, indeed, a bit proud of the fact. Who is there among us who does not respond with sympathetic understanding to the defense of the bride reprimanded for extravagance by her mother-in-law (women have mothers-in-law), "John and I find we can do without the necessities of life. It's the luxuries we must have." One of the obstacles to complete mobilization of our country is extravagance. And at the center of this national failing sits the American woman enthroned.

Europe found it could not allow old-time luxury trades to go on, if the war was to be won. "Business as usual" is not in harmony with victory.

I remember the first time I heard the slogan, and how it carried me and everyone else away. The Zeppelins had visited London the night before. A house in Red Lion Mews was crushed down into its cellar, a heap of ruins. Every pane of glass was shattered in the hospitals surrounding Queen's Square, and ploughed deep, making a great basin in the center of the grass, lay the remnants of the bomb that had buried itself in the heart of England. The shops along Theobald's Road were wrecked, but in the heaps of broken glass in each show window were improvised signs such as, "Don't sympathize with us, buy something." The sign which was displayed oftenest read, "Business as usual."

The first I noticed was in the window of a print shop, the owner a woman. I talked to her through the frame of the shattered glass. She looked very pale and her face was cut, but she and everyone else was calm. And no one was doing business as usual more composedly than a wee tot trudging along to school with a nasty scratch from a glass splinter on her chubby cheek.

"Business as usual" expressed the fine spirit, the courage, the determination of a people. As the sporting motto of an indomitable race, it was very splendid. But war is not a sport, it is a cold, hard science, demanding every energy of the nation for its successful pursuit. In proportion as our indulgence in luxury has been greater than that of any European nation, our challenge to every business must be the more insistent. There must be a straight answer to two questions: Does this enterprise render direct war service, or, if not, is it essential to the well-being of our citizens?

But the discipline will not come from the gods. Nor will our government readily turn taskmaster. The effort must come largely as self-discipline, growing into group determination to win the war and the conviction that it is impossible to achieve victory and conserve the virility of our people, if any considerable part of the community devotes its time, energy and money to creating useless things. A nation can make good in this cataclysm only if it centers its whole power on the two objects in view: military victory, and husbanding of life and resources at home.

Let me hasten to add that the act of creating a thing does not include only the processes of industry. The act of buying is creative. The riot of luxury trades in the United States will not end so long as the American woman remains a steady buyer of luxuries. The mobilization of women as workers is no more essential to the triumph of our cause, than the mobilization of women for thrift. The beginning and end of saving in America rests almost entirely in the hands of women. They are the buyers in the working class and in the professional class. Among the wealthy they set the standard of living.

Practically every appeal for thrift has been addressed to the rich. I am not referring to the supply of channels into which to pour savings, but to appeals to make the economies which will furnish the means to buy stamps or bonds. Those appeals are addressed almost wholly to the well-to-do, as for example, suggestions as to reducing courses at dinner or cutting out "that fourth meal."

Self-denial, no doubt, is supposed to be good for the millionaire soul, but to such it is chiefly recommended, I think, as an example sure of imitation. What the rich do, other women will follow, is the idea. But the steady insistence that we fight in this war for democracy has put into the minds of the people very definite demands for independence and for freedom.

In such a democratic world the newly adopted habits of the wealthy will not prove widely convincing. Economy needs other than an aristocratic stimulus.

How can business be "as usual" when in Paris there are about 1800 of these small workshops where a woman dips Bengal Fire and grenades into a bath of paraffin!

I do not mean to under-estimate the value of economy in the well-to-do class. There is no doubt that shop windows on Fifth Avenue are a severe commentary upon our present intelligence and earnestness of purpose. No one, I think, would deny that it would be a service if the woman of fashion ceased to drape fur here, there and everywhere on her gowns except where she might really need the thick pelt to keep her warm, and instead saved the price of the garment which serves no purpose but that of display, and gave the money in Liberty Bonds to buy a fur-lined coat for some soldier, or food for a starving baby abroad. And overburdened as the railways are with freight and ordinary passenger traffic, I am sure the general public will not fail to appreciate to the full a self-denial which leads patrons of private cars, Pullman and dining coaches to abandon their self-indulgence.

Undoubtedly economy among the rich is of value. I presume few would gainsay that it would have been well for America if the use of private automobiles had long since ceased, and the labor and plants used in their making turned to manufacturing much-needed trucks and ambulances. But while not inclined to belittle the work of any possible saving and self-sacrifice on the part of those of wealth, it seems to me that the most fruitful field for war economy lies among simple people. Thrift waits for democratization.

We of limited means hug some of the most extravagant of habits. The average working-class family enjoys none of the fruits of coöperation We keep each to our isolated family group, while the richer a person is the more does she gather under her roof representatives of other families. Her cook may come from the Berri family, the waitress may be an Andersen, the nurse an O'Hara.

The poor might well practice the economy of fellowship.

The better-off live in apartment houses where the economy of central heating is practised, while the majority of the poor occupy tenements where the extravagance of the individual stove is indulged in. The saving of coal is urged, but the authorities do not seek to secure for the poor the comfort of the true method of fuel saving.

The richer a family is, the more it saves by the use of skilled service. The poor, clinging to their prejudices and refusing to trust one another, do not profit by coöperative buying, or by central kitchens run by experts. Money is wasted by amateurish selection of food and clothing, and nutritive values are squandered by poor cooking.

Unfortunately Uncle Sam does not suggest how many War Saving Stamps could be bought as a result of economy along these lines.

The woman with the pay envelope may democratize thrift. She knows how hard it is to earn money, and has learned to make her wages reach a long way. Then, too, she has it brought home to her each pay day that health is capital. She finds that it is economy to keep well, for lost time brings a light pay envelope. Every woman who keeps herself in condition is making a war saving. There has been no propaganda as yet appealing to women to value dress according to durability and comfort rather than according to its prettiness, to bow to no fashion which means the lessening of power. To corset herself as fashion dictates, to prop herself on high heels, means to a woman just so much lost efficiency, and even the most thoughtless, if appealed to for national saving, might learn to turn by preference in dress, in habits, in recreation, to the simple things.

The Japanese, I am told, make a ceremony of going out from the city to enjoy the beauties of a moonlight night. We go to a stuffy theatre and applaud a night "set." Nature gives her children the one, and the producer charges his patrons for the other. A propaganda of democratic war economy would teach us to delight in the beauties of nature.

In making the change from business as usual to economy, Europe suffered hardship, because although the retrenchments suggested were fairly democratic it had not created channels into which savings might be thrown with certainty of their flowing on to safe expenditures. Europe was not ready with its great thrift schemes, nor had the adjustments been made which would enable a shop to turn out a needed uniform, let us say, in place of a useless dress.

Definite use of savings has been provided for in the United States. The government needs goods of every kind to make our military effort successful. Camps must be built for training the soldiers, uniforms, guns and ammunition supplied. Transportation on land and sea is called for. The government needs money to carry on the industries essential to winning the war.

If a plucky girl who works in a button factory refuses to buy an ornament which she at first thought of getting to decorate her belt, and puts that twenty-five cents into a War Saving Stamp, all in the spirit of backing up her man at the front, she will not find herself thrown out of employment; instead, while demands for unnecessary ornamental fastenings will gradually cease, she will be kept busy on government orders.

Profiting by the errors of those nations who had to blaze out new paths, the United States knit into law, a few months after the declaration of war, not only the quick drafting of its man-power for military service, but methods of absorbing the people's savings. If we neither waste nor hoard, we will not suffer as did Europe from wide-spread unemployment. There is more work to be done than our available labor-power can meet.

There is nothing to fear from the curtailment of luxury; our danger lies in lack of a sound definition of extravagance. Uncle Sam could get more by appeals to simple folk than by homilies preached to the rich. The Great War is a conflict between the ideals of the peoples.

'Tis a people's war, and with women as half the people. The savings made to support the war must needs, then, be made by the people, for the people.

There has been no compelling propaganda to that end. The suggestion of mere "cutting down" may be a valuable goal to set for the well-to-do, but it is not a mark to be hit by those already down to bed rock. The only saving possible to those living on narrow margins is by coöperation, civil or state.

It is a mad extravagance, for instance, to kill with autos children at play in the streets. A saving of life could easily be achieved through group action, by securing children's attendants, by opening play-grounds on the roofs of churches and public buildings, by shutting off streets dedicated to the sacred right of children to play. This would be a war saving touching the heart and the enthusiasm of the people.

Central municipal heating is not a wild dream, but a recognized economy in many places. Municipal kitchens are not vague surmisings, but facts achieved in the towns of Europe. They are forms of war thrift. In America no such converting examples of economy are as yet given, and not an appeal has been made to women to save through solidarity.

Uncle Sam has been commendably quick and wise in offering a reservoir to hold the tiny savings, but slow in starting a democratic propaganda suggesting ways of saving the pennies.

If business as usual is a poor motto, so is life as usual, habits as usual.

X
"AS MOTHER USED TO DO"

Man's admiration for things as mother used to do them is as great an obstacle as business as usual in the path of winning the war and husbanding the race. The glamour surrounding the economic feats of mother in the past hides the shortcomings of today.

I once saw one of her old fortresses, a manor home where in bygone days she had reigned supreme. In the court yard was the smoke house where she cured meat and fish. In the cellar were the caldrons and vats where long ago she tried tallow and brewed beer. And there were all the utensils for dealing with flax. In the garret I saw the spindles for spinning cotton and wool, and the hand looms for weaving the homespun. In her day, mother was a great creator of wealth.

But then an economic earthquake came. Foundations were shaken, the roof was torn off her domestic workshop. Steam and machinery, like cyclones, carried away her industries, and nothing was left to her but odds and ends of occupations.

Toiling in the family circle from the days of the cave dwellers, mother had become so intimately associated in the tribal mind with the hearthstone that the home was called her sphere. Around this segregation accumulated accretions of opinion, layer on layer emanating from the mind of her mate. Let us call the accretions the Adamistic Theory. Its authors happened to be the government and could use the public treasury in furtherance of publicity for their ideas set forth in hieroglyphics cut in stone, or written in plain English and printed on the front page of an American daily.

One of the few occupations left to mother after the disruption of her sphere at the end of the eighteenth century was the preparation of food. In the minds of men, food, from its seed sowing up to its mastication, has always been associated with woman. Mention food and the average man thinks of mother. That is the Adam in him. And so, quite naturally, one must first consider this relation of women to food in the Adamistic Theory.

Countess de Berkaim and her canteen in the Gare de St. Lazarre, Paris.

When the world under war conditions asked to be fed, Adam, running true to his theory, pointed to mother as the source of supply, and declared with an emphasis that came of implicit faith, that the universe need want for nothing, if each woman would eliminate waste in her kitchen and become a voluntary and obedient reflector of the decisions of state and national food authorities. This solution presupposed a highly developed sense of community devotion in women running hand in hand with entire lack of gift for community action. Woman, it was expected, would display more than her proverbial lack of logic by embracing with enthusiasm state direction and at the same time remain an exemplar of individualistic performance. The Adamistic scheme seems still further to demand for its smooth working that the feminine group show self-abnegation and agree that it is not itself suited to reason out general plans.

It is within the range of possibility, however, that no comprehensive scheme of food conservation or effective saving in any line can be imposed on women without consulting them. The negro who agreed "dat de colored folk should keep in dar places," touched a fundamental note in human nature, over-running sex as well as racial boundaries, when he added, "and de colored folk must do de placin'." It might seem to run counter to this bit of wisdom for women to be told that the welfare of the world depends upon them, and then for no woman to be given administrative power to mobilize the group.

But the contest between man's devotion to the habits of his ancestry in the female line, and the ideas of his very living women folk, is as trying to him as it is interesting to the outside observer. The conflicting forces illustrate a universal fact. It is always true that the ruling class, when a discipline and a sacrifice are recognized as necessary, endeavors to make it appear that the new obligation should be shouldered by the less powerful. For instance, to take an illustration quite outside the domestic circle, when America first became convinced that military preparation was incumbent upon us, the ruling class would scarcely discuss conscription, much less adopt universal service. That is, it vetoed self-discipline. In many States, laws were passed putting off upon children in the schools the training which the voting adults knew the nation needed.

In the same way, when food falls short and the victualing of the world becomes a pressing duty, the governing class adopts a thesis that a politically less-favored group can, by saving in small and painful ways, accumulate the extra food necessary to keep the world from starving. The ruling class seeks cover in primitive ideas, accuses Eve of introducing sin into the world, and calls upon her to mend her wasteful ways.

Men, of course, know intellectually that much food is a factory product in these days, but emotionally they have a picture of mother, still supplying the family in a complete, secret, and silent manner.

This Adamistic emotion takes command at the crisis, for when human beings are suddenly faced with a new and agitating situation, primitive ideas seize them. Mother, it is true, did create the goods for immediate consumption, and so the sons of Adam, in a spirit of admiration, doffing their helmets, so to speak, to the primitive woman, turn in this time of stress and call confidently upon Eve's daughters to create and save. The confidence is touching, but perhaps the feminine reaction will not be, and perchance ought not to be just such as Adam expects.

Women have passed in aspiration, and to some extent in action, out of the ultra-individualistic stage of civilization.

The food propaganda reflects the hiatus in Adam's thought. I have looked over hundreds of publications issued by the agricultural departments and colleges of the various States. They tell housewives what to "put into the garbage pail," what to "keep out of the garbage pail," what to substitute for wheat, how to make soap, but, with a single exception, not a word issued suggests to women any saving through group action.

This exception, which stood out as a beacon light in an ocean of literature worthy of the Stone Age, was a small pamphlet issued by the Michigan Agricultural College on luncheons in rural schools. Sound doctrine was preached on the need of the children for substantial and warm noon meals, and the comparative ease and economy with which such luncheons could be provided at the school house. Children can of course be better and more cheaply fed as a group than as isolated units supplied with a cold home-prepared lunch box. And yet with the whole machinery of the state in his hands, Adam's commissions, backed by the people's money, goad mother on to isolated endeavor. She plants and weeds and harvests. She dries and cans, preserves and pickles. Then she calculates and perchance finds that her finished product is not always of the best and has often cost more than if purchased in the open market.

It may be the truest devotion to our Allies to challenge the individualistic rôle recommended by Adam to mother, for it will hinder, not help, the feeding of the world to put women back under eighteenth century conditions. Food is short and expensive because labor is short. And even when the harvest is ripe, the saving of food cannot be set as a separate and commendable goal, and the choice as to where labor shall be expended as negligible. It is a prejudiced devotion to mother and her ways which leads Adam in his food pamphlets to advise that a woman shall sit in her chimney corner and spend time peeling a peach "very thin," when hundreds of bushels of peaches rot in the orchards for lack of hands to pick them.

Just how wide Adam's Eve has opened the gate of Eden and looked out into the big world is not entirely clear, but probably wide enough to glimpse the fact that all the advice Adam has recently given to her runs counter to man's method of achievement. Men have preached to one another for a hundred years and more and practiced so successfully the concentration in industry of unlimited machinery with a few hands, that even mother knows some of the truths in regard to the creation of wealth in the business world, and she is probably not incapable of drawing a conclusion from her own experience in the transfer of work from the home to the factory.

If they are city dwellers, women have seen bread and preserves transferred; if farm dwellers, they have seen the curing of meat and fish transferred, the making of butter and cheese. They know that because of this transfer the home is cleaner and quieter, more people better fed and clothed, and the hours of the factory worker made shorter than those "mother used to work." With half an eye women cannot fail to note that the labor which used to be occupied in the home in interminable hours of spinning, baking and preserving, has come to occupy itself for regulated periods in the school, in business, in factory or cannery. And lo, Eve finds herself with a pay envelope able to help support the quieter, cleaner home!

All this is a commonplace to the business man, who knows that the evolution has gone so far that ten percent of the married women of America are in gainful pursuits, and that capital ventured on apartment hotels brings a tempting return.

But the Adamistic theory is based on the dream that women are contentedly and efficiently conducting in their flats many occupations, and longing to receive back into the life around the gas-log all those industries which in years gone by were drawn from the fireside and established as money making projects in mill or work-shop. And so Adam addresses an exhortation to his Eve: "Don't buy bread, bake it; don't buy flour, grind your own; don't buy soap, make it; don't buy canned, preserved, or dried food, carry on the processes yourself; don't buy fruits and vegetables, raise them."

Not a doubt seems to exist in Adam's mind as to the efficiency of functioning woman-power in this way. According to the Adamistic theory, work as mother used to do it is unqualifiedly perfect. This flattering faith is naturally balm to women's hearts, and yet there are skeptics among them. When quite by themselves women speculate as to how much of the fruit and vegetables now put up in the home will "work."

They smile when the hope is expressed that the quality will rise above the old-time domestic standard. The home of the past was a beehive in which women drudged, and little children were weary toilers, and the result was not of a high grade. Statistics have shown that seventy-five percent of the home-made bread of America was a poor product. I lived as a child in the days of home-made bread. Once in so often the batch of bread "went sour," and there seemed to be an unfailing supply of stale bread which "must be eaten first." Those who cry out against a city of bakers' bread, have never lived in a country of the home-made loaf. It is the Adamistic philosophy, so complimentary to Eve, that leads us to expect that all housewives can turn out a product as good as that of an expert who has specialized to the one end of making bread, and who is supplied with expensive equipment beyond the reach of the individual to possess. But there are rebellious consumers who point out that the baker is under the law, while the housewife is a law unto herself. Against the baker's shortcomings such brave doubters assure us we have redress, we can refuse to patronize him; against the housewife there is no appeal, her family must swallow her product to the detriment of digestion.

It may be the brutal truth, taking bread as the index, that only a quarter of the processes carried on in the home turn out satisfactorily, while of the other three-quarters, a just verdict may show that mother gets a "little too much lye" in the soap, cooks the preserves a "little too hard," "candies the fruit just a little bit," and grinds the flour in the mill "not quite fine enough."

But perhaps even more than the quality of the product does the question of the economical disposition of labor-power agitate some women. They are asking, since labor is very scarce, whether the extreme individualistic direction of their labor-power is permissible. The vast majority of American homes are without servants. In those homes are the women working such short hours that they can, without dropping important obligations, take over preserving, canning, dehydrating, the making of bread, soap, and butter substitute? Has the tenement-house dweller accommodation suitable for introducing these industrial processes into her home? Would the woman in the small ménage in the country be wise in cutting down time given, for instance, to the care of her baby and to reading to the older children, and using the precious moments laboriously to grind wheat to flour? My observation convinces me that conscientious housewives in servantless or one-servant households, with work adjusted to a given end, with relative values already determined upon, are not prepared by acceptance of the Adamistic theory to return to primitive occupations.

But even if business and home life could respond to the change without strain, even if both could easily turn back on the road they have come during the last hundred years, commerce yielding up and the home re-adopting certain occupations, we should carefully weigh the economic value of a reversion to primitive methods.

The Adamistic attitude is influenced, perhaps unconsciously but no less certainly, by the fact that the housewife is an unpaid worker. If an unpaid person volunteers to do a thing, it is readily assumed that the particular effort is worth while. "We get the labor for nothing" puts to rout all thought of valuation. No doubt Adam will have to give over thinking in this loose way. Labor-power, whether it is paid for or not, must be used wisely or we shall not be able to maintain the structure of our civilization.

Then, too, the Adamistic theory weighs and values the housewife's time as little as it questions the quality of the home product. Any careful reader of the various "Hints to Housewives" which have appeared, will note that the "simplifying of meals" recommended would require nearly double the time to prepare. The simplification takes into consideration only the question of food substitutions, price and waste. Mother is supposed to be wholly or largely unemployed and longing for unpaid toil. Should any housewife

---

conscientiously follow the advice given her by state and municipal authorities she would be the drudge at the center of a home quite medieval in development.

Let us take a concrete example:--In a recently published and widely applauded cookbook put out by a whole committee of Adamistic philosophers, it is stated that the object of the book is to give practical hints as to the various ways in which "economies can be effected and waste saved;" and yet no saving of the woman's time, nerves and muscles is referred to from cover to cover. The housewife is told, for instance, to "insist upon getting the meat trimmings." The fat "can be rendered." And then follows the process in soap-making. Mother is to place the scraps of fat on the back of the stove. If she "watches it carefully" and does not allow it to get hot enough to smoke there will be no odor. No doubt if she removes her watchful eye and turns to bathe her baby, her tenement will reek with smoking fat. She is to pursue this trying of fat and nerves day by day until she has six pounds of grease. Next, she is to "stir it well," cool it, melt it again; she is then to pour in the lye, "slowly stirring all the time." Add ammonia. Then "stir the mixture constantly for twenty minutes or half an hour."

In contrast to all this primeval elaboration is the simple, common-sense rule: Do not buy the trimmings, make the butcher trim meat before weighing, insist that soap-making shall not be brought back to defile the home, but remain where it belongs, a trade in which the workers can be protected by law, and its malodorousness brought under regulation.

In the same spirit the Adamistic suggestion to Eve to save coal by a "heatless day" is met by the cold challenge of the riotous extravagance of cooking in twelve separate tenements, twelve separate potatoes, on twelve separate fires.

The Adamistic theory, through its emphasis on the relation of food to Eve, and the almost religious necessity of its manipulation at the altar of the home cook-stove, has drawn thought away from the nutritive side of what we eat. While the child in the streets is tossing about such words as calories and carbohydrates with a glibness that comes of much hearing, physiology and food values are destined to remain as far away as ever from the average family breakfast table. Segregating a sex in the home, it is true, centralizes it in a given place, but it does not necessarily train the individual to function efficiently. Mother, as she "used to do," cooks by rule of thumb; in fact, how could she do otherwise, since she must keep one eye on her approving Adam while the other eye glances at the oven. The Adamistic theory requires individualistic action, and disapproves specialization in Eve.

The theory also demands economic dependence in the home builder. Mother's labor is not her own, she lives under the truck system, so to speak. She is paid in kind for her work. Influenced by the Adamistic theory, the human animal is the only species in which sex and economic relations are closely linked, the only one in which the female depends upon the male for sustenance. Mother must give personal service to those about her, and in return the law ensures her keep according to the station of her husband, that is, not according to her ability or usefulness, but according to the man's earning capacity.

The close association of mother with home in the philosophy of her mate, has circumscribed her most natural and modest attempts at relaxation. Mother's holiday is a thing to draw tears from those who contemplate it. The summer outing means carrying the family from one spot to another, and making the best of new surroundings for the old group. The "day off" means a concentration of the usual toil into a few hours, followed by a hazy passing show that she is too weary to enjoy. The kindly farmer takes his wife this year to the county fair. She's up at four to "get on" with the work. She serves breakfast, gives the children an extra polish in honor of the day, puts on the clean frocks and suits with an admonition "not to get all mussed up" before the start. The farmer cheerily counsels haste in order that "we may have a good long day of it." He does not say what "it" is, but the wife knows. At last the house is ready to be left, and the wife and her brood are ready to settle down in the farm wagon.

The fair grounds are reached. Adam has prepared the setting. It has no relation to mother's needs. It was a most thrilling innovation when in the summer of 1914 the Women's Political Union first set up big tents at county fairs, fitted with comfortable chairs for mother, and cots and toys, nurses and companions for the children. The farmer's wife for the first time was relieved of care, and could go off to see the sights with her mind at rest, if she desired anything more active than rocking lazily with the delicious sensation of having nothing to do.

Women must not blame Adam for lack of thoughtfulness. He cannot put himself in mother's place. She must do her own thinking or let women who are capable of thought do it for her.

Men are relieved when mother is independent and happy. The farmer approved the crèche tent at the county fairs. It convinced him that women have ideas to contribute to the well-being of the community. The venture proved the greatest of vote getters for the suffrage referendum.

In fact, men themselves are the chief opponents of the Adamistic theory to-day. The majority want women to organize the home and it is only a small minority who place obstacles in the way of the wider functioning of women. It is Eve herself who likes to exaggerate the necessity of her personal service. I have seen many a primitive housewife grow hot at the suggestion that her methods need modifying. It seemed like severing the silken cords by which she held her mate, to challenge her pumpkin pie.

But women are slowly overcoming Eve. Take the item of the care of children in city parks. The old way is for fifty women to look after fifty separate children, and thus waste the time of some thirty of them in keeping fifty miserable children in segregation. The new way, now successfully initiated, is to form play groups of happy children under the leadership of capable young women trained for such work.

Salvaging New York City's food waste was a very splendid bit of coöperative action on the part of women. Mrs. William H. Lough of the Women's University Club found on investigation that thousands of tons of good food are lost by a condemnation, necessarily rough and ready, by the Board of Health. She secured permission to have the sound and unsound fruits and vegetables separated and with a large committee of women saved the food for consumption by the community by dehydrating and other preserving processes.

This was not as mother used to do.

Mother's ways are being investigated and discarded the whole world round. At last accounts half the population of Hamburg was being fed through municipal kitchens and in Great Britain an order has been issued by Lord Rhondda, the Food Controller, authorizing local authorities to open kitchens as food distributing centers. The central government is to bear twenty-five percent of the cost of equipment and lend another twenty-five percent to start the enterprise.

Mother's cook stove cannot bear the strain of war economies.

Dropping their old segregation, women are going forth in fellowship with men to meet in new ways the pressing problems of a new world.

XI
A LAND ARMY

Great Britain, France and Germany have mobilized a land army of women; will the United States do less? Not if the farmer can be brought to have as much faith in American women as the women have in themselves. And why should they not have faith; the farm has already tested them out, and they have not been found wanting. In face of this fine accomplishment the minds of some men still entertain doubt, or worse, obliviousness, to the possible contribution of women to land service.

The farmer knows his need and has made clear statement of the national dilemma in the form of a memorial to the President of the United States. In part, it is as follows:

"If food is to win the war, as we are assured on every side, the farmers of America must produce more food in 1918 than they did in 1917. Under existing conditions we cannot equal the production of 1917, much less surpass it, and this for reasons over which the farmers have no control. "The chief causes which will inevitably bring about a smaller crop next year, unless promptly removed by national action, are six in number, of which the first is the shortage of farm labor.

"Since the war began in 1914 and before the first draft was made there is reason to believe that more farm workers had left farms than there are men in our army and navy together. Those men were drawn away by the high wages paid in munition plants and other war industries, and their places remain unfilled. In spite of the new classification, future drafts will still further reduce the farm labor supply."

With a million and a half men drawn out of the country and ten billion dollars to be expended on war material, making every ammunition factory a labor magnet, it seems like the smooth deceptions of prestidigitation to answer the cry of the farmer with suggestion that men rejected by the draft or high school boys be paroled to meet the exigency. The farm can't be run with decrepit men or larking boys, nor the war won with less than its full quota of soldiers. Legislators, government officials and farm associations by sudden shifting of labor battalions cannot camouflage the fact that the front line trenches of the fighting army and labor force are undermanned.

Women can and will be the substitutes if the experiments already made are signs of the times.

Groups of women from colleges and seasonal trades have ploughed and harrowed, sowed and planted, weeded and cultivated, mowed and harvested, milked and churned, at Vassar, Bryn Mawr and Mount Holyoke, at Newburg and Milton, at Bedford Hills and

Mahwah. It has been demonstrated that our girls from college and city trade can do farm work, and do it with a will. And still better, at the end of the season their health wins high approval from the doctors and their work golden opinions from the farmers.

Twelve crusaders were chosen from the thirty-three students who volunteered for dangerous service during a summer vacation on the Vassar College farm. The twelve ventured out on a new enterprise that meant aching muscles, sunburn and blisters, but not one of the twelve "ever lost a day" in their eight hours at hard labor, beginning at four-thirty each morning for eight weeks during one of our hottest summers. They ploughed with horses, they ploughed with tractors, they sowed the seed, they thinned and weeded the plants, they reaped, they raked, they pitched the hay, they did fencing and milking. The Vassar farm had bumper crops on its seven hundred and forty acres, and its superintendent, Mr. Louis P. Gillespie, said, "A very great amount of the work necessary for the large production was done by our students. They hoed and cultivated sixteen acres of field corn, ten acres of ensilage corn, five acres of beans, five acres of potatoes; carried sheaves of rye and wheat to the shocks and shocked them; and two of the students milked seven cows at each milking time. In the garden they laid out a strawberry bed of two thousand plants, helped to plant corn and beans, picked beans and other vegetables. They took great interest in the work and did the work just as well as the average man and made good far beyond the most sanguine expectations."

At first the students were paid twenty-five cents an hour, the same rate as the male farm hands. The men objected, saying that the young women were beginners, but by the end of the summer the critics realized that "brains tell" and said the girls were worth the higher wage, though they had only been getting, in order to appease the masculine prejudice, seventeen and a half cents an hour. There is no pleasing some people! If women are paid less, they are unfair competitors, if they are paid equally they are being petted--in short, fair competitors.

Mt. Holyoke and Bryn Mawr have made experiments, and, like Vassar, demonstrated not only that women can, and that satisfactorily, work on the land, but that they will, and that cheerfully. The groups were happy and they comprehended that they were doing transcendently important work, were rendering a patriotic service by filling up the places left vacant by the drafted men.

The Women's Agricultural Camp, known popularly as the "Bedford Unit," proved an experiment rich in practical suggestion. Barnard students, graduates of the Manhattan Trade School, and girls from seasonal trades formed the backbone of the group. They were housed in an old farmhouse, chaperoned by one of the Barnard professors, fed by student dietitians from the Household Arts Department of Teachers College, transported from farm to farm by seven chauffeurs, and coached in the arts of Ceres by an agricultural expert. The "day laborers" as well as the experts were all women.

An agricultural unit, in the uniform approved by the Woman's Land Army of America.

In founding the camp Mrs. Charles W. Short, Jr., had three definite ideas in mind. First, she was convinced that young women could without ill-effect on their health, and should as a patriotic service, do all sorts of agricultural work. Second, that in the present crisis the opening up of new land with women as farm managers is not called for, but rather the supply of the labor-power on farms already under cultivation is the need. Third, that the women laborers must, in groups, have comfortable living conditions without being a burden on the farmer's wife, must have adequate pay, and must have regulated hours of work.

With these sound ideas as its foundation the camp opened at Mt. Kisco, backed by the Committee on Agriculture of the Mayor's Committee of Women on National Defense of New York City, under the chairmanship of Virginia Gildersleeve, Dean of Barnard College.

At its greatest enrolment the unit had seventy-three members. When the prejudice of the fanners was overcome, the demand for workers was greater than the camp could supply. Practically the same processes were carried through as at Vassar, and the verdict of the farmer on his new helpers was that "while less strong than men, they more than made up for this by superior conscientiousness and quickness." Proof of the genuineness of his estimate was shown in his willingness to pay the management of the camp the regulation two dollars for an eight hour working day. And it indicated entire satisfaction with the experiment, rather than abstract faith in woman, that each farmer anxiously urged the captain of the group at the end of his first trial to "please bring the same young ladies tomorrow." He was sure no others so good existed.

The unit plan seems a heaven-born solution of many of the knotty problems of the farm. In the first place, the farmer gets cheerful and handy helpers, and his over-worked wife does not find her domestic cares added to in the hot summer season. The new hands house and feed themselves. From the point of view of the worker, the advantage is that her food at the camp is prepared by trained hands and the proverbial farm isolation gives way to congenial companionship.

These separate experiments growing out of the need of food production and the shortage of labor have brought new blood to the farm, have turned the college girl on vacation and, what is more important, being a solution of an industrial problem, the unemployed in seasonal trades, into recruits for an agricultural army. And by concentrating workers in well-run camps there has been attracted to the land a higher order of helper.

One obstacle in the way of the immediate success of putting such women on the land is a wholly mistaken idea in the minds of many persons of influence in agricultural matters that the new labor can be diverted to domestic work in the farm house. This view is urged in the following letter to me from the head of one of our best agricultural colleges: "The farm labor shortage is much more acute than is generally understood and I have much confidence in the possibility of a great amount of useful work in food production being done by women who are physically strong enough and who can secure sufficient preliminary training to do this with some degree of efficiency. Probably the larger measure of service could be done by relieving women now on the farms of this State from the double burden of indoor work and the attempt to assist in farm operations and chores. If farm women would get satisfactory domestic assistance within the house they could add much to the success of field husbandry. Women who know farm conditions and who could largely take the place of men in the management of outdoor affairs can accomplish much more than will ever be possible by drafting city-bred women directly into garden or other forms of field work."

The opinions expressed in this letter are as generally held as they are mistaken. In the first place, the theory that the country-bred woman in America is stronger and healthier than the city-bred has long since been exploded. The assumption cannot stand up under the facts. Statistics show that the death rate in the United States is lower in city than in farm communities, and if any added proof were needed to indicate that the stamina of city populations overbalances the country it was furnished by the draft records. Any group of college and Manhattan Trade School girls could be pitted against a group of women from the farms and win the laurels in staying powers. Nor must it be overlooked that we are not dealing here with uncertainties; the mettle of the girls has been proved.

In any case the fact must be faced that these agricultural units will not do domestic work. Nine-tenths of the farm houses in America are without modern conveniences. The well-appointed barn may have running water, but the house has not. To undertake work as a domestic helper on the average farm is to step back into quite primitive conditions. The farmer's wife can attract no one from city life, where so much cooperation is enjoyed, to her extreme individualistic surroundings.

A second obstacle to the employment of this new labor-force is due to the government's failure to see the possibility of saving most valuable labor-power and achieving an economic gain by dovetailing the idle months of young women in industrial life into the rush time of agriculture.

One department suggests excusing farm labor from the draft, as if we had already fulfilled our obligation in man-power to the battlefront of our Allies. The United States Senate discusses bringing in coolie and contract labor, as if we had not demonstrated our unfitness to deal with less advanced peoples, and as if a republic could live comfortably with a class of disfranchised workers. The Labor Department declares it will mobilize for the farm an army of a million boys, as if the wise saw, "boys will be boys," did not apply with peculiar sharpness of flavor to the American vintage, God bless them, and as if it were not our plain duty at this world crisis to spur up rather than check civilizing agencies and keep our boys in school for the full term.

Refusing to be in the least crushed by government neglect, far-seeing women determined to organize widely and carefully their solution of the farm-labor problem. To this end the Women's National Farm and Garden Association, the Garden Clubs of America, the Young Women's Christian Association, the Woman's Suffrage Party, the New York Women's University Club, and the Committee of the Women's Agricultural Camp, met with representatives of the Grange, of the Cornell Agricultural College, and of the Farmingdale State School of Agriculture, and formed an advisory council, the object of which is to "stimulate the formation of a Land Army of Women to take the places on the farms of the men who are being drafted for active service." This is to be on a nationwide scale.

The Council has put lecturers in the Granges to bring to the farmer by the spoken word and lantern slides the value of the labor of women, and is appealing to colleges, seasonal trades and village communities to form units for the Land Army. It is asking the coöperation of the labor bureaus to act as media through which units may be placed where labor is most needed.

This mobilization of woman-power is not yet large or striking. The effort is entirely civil. But all the more is it praiseworthy. It shows on the part of women, clear-eyed recognition of facts as they exist and vision as to the future.

The mobilization of this fresh labor-power should of course be taken in hand by the government. Not only that, it should be led by women as in Great Britain and Germany. But the spirit in America today is the same as in England the first year of the war,--a disposition to exclude women from full service.

But facts remain facts in spite of prejudice, and the Woman's Land Army, with faith and enthusiasm in lieu of a national treasury, are endeavoring to bring woman-power and the untilled fields together. The proved achievement of the individual worker will win the employer, the unit plan with its solution of housing conditions and dreary isolation will overcome not only the opposition of the farmer's wife, but that of the intelligent worker. When the seed time of the movement has been lived through by anxious and inspired women, the government may step in to reap the harvest of a nation's gratitude.

The mobilization of woman-power on the farm is the need of the hour, and the wise and devoted women who are trying to answer the need, deserve an all-hail from the people of the United States and her Allies.

XII
WOMAN'S PART IN SAVING CIVILIZATION

Men have played--all honor to them--the major part in the actual conflict of the war. Women will mobilize for the major part of binding up the wounds and conserving civilization.

The spirit of the world might almost be supposed to have been looking forward to this day and clearly seeing its needs, so well are women being prepared to receive and carry steadily the burden which will be laid on their shoulders. For three-quarters of a century schools and colleges have given to women what they had to confer in the way of discipline. Gainful pursuits were opened up to them, adding training in ordered occupation and self-support. Lastly has come the Great War, with its drill in sacrifice and economy, its larger opportunities to function and achieve, its ideals of democracy which have directly and quickly led to the political enfranchisement of women in countries widely separated.

Fate has prepared women to share fully in the saving of civilization.

Whether victory be ours in the immediate future, or whether the dangers rising so clearly on the horizon develop into fresh alignments leading to years of war, civilization stands in jeopardy. Political ideals and ultimate social aims may remain intact, but the immediate, practical maintenance of those standards of life which are necessary to ensure strong and fruitful reactions are in danger of being swept away.

We have been destroying the life, the wealth and beauty of the world. The nobility of our aim in the war must not blind us to the awfulness and the magnitude of the destruction. In the fighting forces there are at least thirty-eight million men involved in international or civil conflict. Over four million men have fallen, and three million have been maimed for life. Disease has taken its toll of fighting strength and economic power. In addition to all this human depletion, we have the loss of life and the destruction of health and initiative in harried peoples madly flying across their borders from invading armies.

Starvation has swept across wide areas, and steady underfeeding rules in every country in Europe and in the cities of America, letting loose malnutrition, that hidden enemy whose ambushes are more serious than the attacks of an open foe. The world is sick.

And the world is poor. The nations have spent over a hundred billions on the war, and that is but part of the wealth which has gone down in the catastrophe. Thousands of square miles are plowed so deep with shot and shell and trench that the fertile soil lies buried beneath unyielding clay. Orchards and forests are gone.

Villages are wiped out, cities are but skeletons of themselves. In the face of all the need of reconstruction we must admit, however much we would wish to cover the   fact,--the   world   is   poor.

A useful blending of Allied women. Miss Kathleen Burke (Scotch) exhibiting the X-ray ambulance equipped by Mrs. Ayrlon (English) and Madame Curie (French)

And still, as in no other war, the will to guard human welfare has remained dominant. The country rose to a woman in most spirited fashion to combat the plan to lower the standards of labor conditions in the supposed interest of war needs. With but few exceptions the States have strengthened their labor laws. In its summary the American Association for Labor Legislation says:

"Eleven States strengthened their child labor laws, by raising age limits, extending restrictions to new employments, or shortening hours. Texas passed a new general statute setting a fifteen-year minimum age for factories and Vermont provided for regulations in conformity with those of the Federal Child Labor Act. Kansas and New Hampshire legislated on factory safeguards, Texas on fire escapes, New Jersey on scaffolds, Montana on electrical apparatus, Delaware on sanitary equipment, and West Virginia on mines. New Jersey forbade the manufacture of articles of food or children's wear in tenements.

"Workmen's compensation laws were enacted in Delaware, Idaho, New Mexico, South Dakota, and Utah, making forty States and Territories which now have such laws, in addition to the Federal Government's compensation law, for its own half-million civilian employees. In more than twenty additional States existing acts were amended, the changes being marked by a tendency to extend the scope, shorten the working period, and increase provision for medical care."

The Great War, far from checking the movement for social welfare, has quickened the public sense of responsibility. That fact opens the widest field to women for work in which they are best prepared by nature and training.

Many keen thinkers are concerned over the question of population. One of our most distinguished professors has thrown out a hint of a possibility that considering the greater proportion of women to men some form of plurality of wives may become necessary. The disturbed balance of the sexes is a thing that will right itself in one generation. Need of population will be best answered by efforts to salvage the race. The United States loses each year five hundred thousand babies under twelve months of age from preventable causes. An effort to save them would seem more reasonable than a demand for more children to neglect. Life will be so full of drive and interest, that the woman who has given no hostages to fortune will find ample scope for her powers outside of motherhood. The "old maid" of tomorrow will have a mission more honored and important than was hers in the past.

But whatever the conclusions as to the wisest method of building up population, there is no doubt that government and individuals will make strict valuation of the essentials and non-essentials in national life. In our poverty we will test all things in the light of their benefit to the race and hold fast that which is good.

The opinions of women will weigh in this national accounting. There will be no money to squander, and women to a unit will stand behind those men who think a recreation field is of more value than a race track. It will be the woman's view, there being but one choice, that it is better to encourage fleetness and skill in boys and girls than in horses. If we have just so much money to spend and the question arises as to whether there shall be corner saloons or municipal kitchens, public sentiment, made in good measure by women, will eschew the saloon.

The things that lend themselves to the husbanding of the race will draw as a magnet those who have borne the race. The tired world will need for its rejuvenation a broadened and deepened medical science. Women are too wise to permit sanitation and research to fall to a low level. On the contrary, they will wish them to be more thorough. There will be economy along the less essential lines to meet the cost.

The flagging spirit needs the inspiration of art and music. To secure them in the future, state and municipal effort will be demanded. Women are born economizers. They have been trained to pinch each penny. With their advent into political life, roads and public buildings will cost less. Through careful saving, funds will be made available for the things of the spirit.

One of the men conductors on the New York street railways somewhat reproachfully remarked to me, "No one ever came to look at the recreation room and restaurant at the car barns until women were taken on. Men don't seem to count." Is the reproach deserved? Have women been narrow in sympathy? Perhaps we have assumed that men can look out for themselves. They could, but in private life they never do. Women have to do the mothering. A trade-unionist is ready enough to regulate wages and hours, but he gives not a thought to surroundings in factory and workshop.

An act of protection generally starts with solicitude about a woman or child. Factory legislation took root in their needs. There was no mercy for the man worker. His only chance of getting better conditions was when women entered his occupation, and the regulation meant for her benefit indirectly served his interest.

"Men suffer more than women in certain dangerous trades, but I did not suppose you were generous enough to care anything about them," came in answer to an inquiry at a labor conference at the end of a most admirable paper on women in dangerous trades, given by one of the doctors in the New York City Department of Health. He was speaking to an audience of working women. I doubt if his hearers had given a thought to men workers.

Perhaps this is natural, since there has been going on at the same time with the development of factory legislation in America a strong propaganda directed especially at political freedom for women. We have been laying stress on the wrongs of woman and demanding very persistently and convincingly her rights. The industrial needs and rights of the man have been overlooked.

With increasing numbers of women entering the industrial world, with ever widening extension of the vote to women, and the consequent quickening of public responsibility, together with the recent experience of Europe demonstrating the importance of care for all workers, both men and women, there is ground for hope that even the United States, where protective legislation is so retarded in development, will enter upon wide and fundamental plans for conservation of all our human resources.

Protection of the worker, housing conditions, the feeding of factory employees and school children, play grounds and recreation centers, will challenge the world for first consideration. These are the social processes which command most surely the hearts and minds of women. The churning which the war has given humanity has roused in women a realization that upon them rests at least half the burden of saving civilization from wreck. Here is the world, with such and such needs for food, clothing, shelter, with such and such needs for sanitation, hospitals, and above all, for education, for science, for the arts, if it is not to fall back into the conditions of the Middle Ages. How can women aid in making secure the national position? Certainly not by idleness, inefficiency, an easy policy of laissez faire. They must labor, economize, and pool their brains.

Women can save civilization only by the broadest coöperative action, by daring to think, by daring to be themselves. The world is entering an heroic age calling for heroic women.

APPENDIX

DOCUMENTS USED IN WOMEN'S WAR-WORK IN ENGLAND AND FRANCE

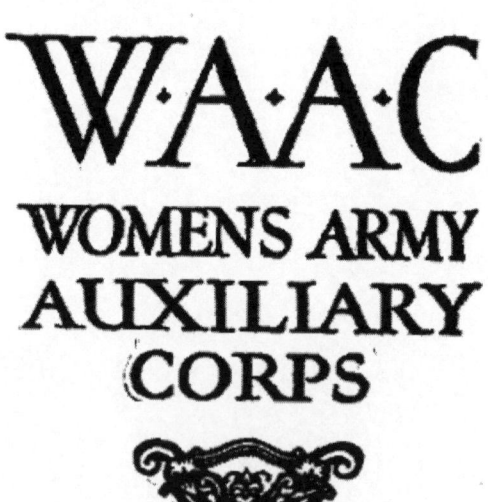

CONFIDENTIAL. Reference No: J.W. 21 [o.]

Joint Woman's V.A.D. Department.

DEVONSHIRE HOUSE. PICCADILLY, LONDON. W.I.

Return to Secretary, V.A.D Department. Devonshire House, Piccadilly, S.W.I.

Territorial Force Associations, British Red Cross Society. Order of St. John of Jerusalem.

Telegrams [unreadable] Telephone Mayfair 4707

B.R.C.S. or Order of St. John ...

Sir,

Will you kindly fill up the following form of Medical Certificate, returning it to the address given above.

Your communication will be received as strictly confidential.

It is urgently requested that Members' names and detachment numbers should be filled in legibly.

Yours faithfully,

MARGARET HEMPHILL

MEDICAL CERTIFICATE

1. Name

2. County   No. of Detachment

3. How long have you been acquainted with her?

4. Have you attended her professionally?

5. For what complaint?

6. Is she intelligent and of active habits?

7. General health?

8. Has she flat feet, hammer-toe, or any other defect?

9. Is her vision good in each eye?

10. Is her hearing perfect?

11. Has she sound teeth, and if not, have they been properly attended to by a Dentist lately?

12. Has she shown any tendency to Rheumatism, Anaemia, Tuberculosis, or other illness?

13. When?

14. What?

15. Has she ever had influenza?

16. Does she suffer from headaches?

17. Any form of fits?

18. Heart disease or varicose veins?

19. Is she subject to any functional disturbance?

I have on the .... day of 191....
seen and examined .... and hereby
certify that she is apparently in good health, that she is
not labouring under any deformity, and is, in my
opinion, both physically and mentally competent to
undertake duty in a Military Hospital, and is
[*]A. Fit for General Service.
  B. Fit for Home Service only.
  C. Unfit.

Date (Signed)   *Address*

[*] Kindly delete categories which do not apply.

Reference No.: J.W. 19c.

JOINT WOMEN'S V.A.D. DEPARTMENT. Territorial Forces Association. British Red Cross Society. Order of St. John of Jerusalem. DEVONSHIRE HOUSE, PICCADILLY, LONDON. W1.

QUALIFICATIONS of Members of Women's Voluntary Aid Detachments for Nursing Service or General Service.

---

1. (a) Name in full (*Mrs. or Miss*).   (b) If Married state Maiden Name.

2. Permanent Postal Address.   Present Postal Address.

3. Telephone No.

4. Telegraphic Address.

5. Detachment County and No.   B.R.C.S.
St. John Brigade.
St. John Association.

6. Name and Address of Commandant of Detachment.

7. Rank in Detachment.

8. Time of Service in Detachment.

9. Age and Date of Birth.

10. Place and Country of Birth.

11. Nationality at Birth.

12. Present Nationality.

13. Height.

14. Weight.

15. Where Educated.

16. At what age did you leave school?

17. Whether Single, Married, or Widow.

18. If not Single, state Nationality of Husband.

19. Name and Address of Next-of-Kin or Nearest Relation residing in the British Isles.

20. Father's Nationality at Birth.

21. Mother's Nationality at Birth.

22. Father's Profession.

23. Religion.

24. (a) If you volunteer for nursing duties state what experience you have had in wards.
   (b) Name and address of hospital.
   (c) Date.

25. Certificates held.

26. (a) Nursing.   (f) Motor Driver.
    (b) Kitchen.   (g) Laboratory Attendant.
    (c) Clerical.   (h) X-Ray Attendant.
    (d) Storekeeping.   (i) House Work.
    (e) Dispenser.   (j) Pantry Work.

27. State what experience and qualifications you have had   for Categories in No. 26.

28. Have you been inoculated against Enteric Fever?   If so, what date?
   If not, are you willing to be?
   Have you been vaccinated?
   It so, what date?
   If not, are you willing to be?

29. Your usual Occupation or Profession?
   Your present Occupation or Profession?

30. Give the Names and Addresses of two British Householders with permanent addresses in the British Isles who have known applicant for two or more years,

but are not related to applicant, to act as References, having previously obtained their permission to use their names.

(a) (Mayor, Magistrate, Justice of the Peace, Minister of Religion,
Barrister, Physician, Solicitor or Notary Public).
Acquaintance dating from year _____

(b) Lady.
Acquaintance dating from year _____

31. Name and Address of Head of College or School, recent Business   Employer, Head of Government Department, Secretary of Society or some other person who can be referred to for a report on your qualifications for the work selected. (The Quartermaster of your V.A.D. could be given if you have worked in her department.)
In what capacity employed?
How long employed?
Year?

32. Are you willing to serve at home or abroad?

33. Are you willing to serve in Civil Hospitals from which   personnel have been withdrawn for War Service?

34. Are you willing to serve:--
(a) With pay,

(b) For expenses only,
on the terms of service laid down in our terms of
service?

N. B.--Members who can afford to work for their
expenses only are urgently needed.

35. Date after which you will be available for duty.

36. (a) Are you pledged to serve in any other
organisation?   (b) If so, what?

37. (a) Have you served with the Women's Legion
or any   similar organisation?
   (b) If so, what?

I hereby declare that the above statements are
complete and correct to the best of my knowledge and
belief.

Date .... Usual Signature ....

For Office Purposes, please add your full Christian
Names and Surname legibly written.

I certify that the above declaration is, to the best of
my knowledge and belief, true; and that M .... is a
fit and proper person to be employed by the Joint
V.A.D. Committee.

REMARKS:--

Date .... Signed ....
Commandant.

Date .... Countersigned
.... *County Director.*

NOTE.--Commandants are held responsible for all statements on this form being accurate so far as it is possible for them to find out, also for the fact that the member who signs it is a British subject, and in every way suitable for appointment by the Joint V.A.D. Committee.

This form must be signed by the Commandant, who should then send it to the County Director for counter signature and forwarding to Headquarters.

Application No.

For Official use only.

CONFIDENTIAL.

WOMEN'S ARMY AUXILIARY CORPS FORM OF APPLICATION

N.B.--No woman need apply who is not prepared to offer her services for the duration of the war and to take up work wherever she is required.

1. Name in Full (Mrs. or Miss).

2. Permanent Postal Address.

2a. State nearest Railway Station.

3. Surname at birth, if different.

4. For what work do you offer your services? State your   qualifications for this work. (The occupations for which women are
   required are set out in the accompanying leaflet.)

5. Are you willing to serve:--
(a) At Home and Abroad as may be required.
(b) At Home only.

6. If selected and enrolled how many days' notice will you require before   your services are available?

7. Age and date of birth.

8. Place and Country of Birth.

9. Nationality at Birth.

10. Present Nationality   (if naturalised give date).

11. Whether single, married or widow.   If married state number of children,
    (a) under 12 years old.
    (b) "   5 "   "

12. If not single state Nationality of Husband.
(a) Is your husband serving with the Forces?
    (b) If so, where?

13. Father's Nationality at Birth.

14. Mother's Nationality at Birth.

15. Father's Occupation.

16. State school or college where educated.   At what age did you leave School?

17. Particulars of any other Training, stating Certificates held.

18. (a) Name and Address of your present employer   (*see Note on other side*).
    N.B.--(The employer will not be referred to unless he is given as a
    reference under paragraph 20 below.)

(b) Nature of his business.

(c) Capacity in which you are employed.

(d) Length of your service with him.

(e) Salary which you are now receiving.

19. Previous business experience (if any) giving dates, salaries   received, and names of Employers.

20. Give below for purposes of reference the names of two or more British householders with their permanent addresses, one of whom should be, if possible, your present or previous Employer, a Teacher, a Town Councillor, Mayor or Provost, Justice of Peace, Minister of Religion, Doctor or Solicitor, who has known you for two or more years, but is not related to you. One of the references must be a woman.

(a) Name.
Profession or Occupation.
Address.
(b) Name.
Profession or Occupation.
Address.
(c) Name.
Profession or Occupation.
Address.

An offer of Service can in no way be regarded as a final enrolment.

I hereby declare that the above statements are complete and correct to the best of my knowledge and belief.

Date _____ *Usual Signature* _____

This Form should be filled in by the Applicant and returned to:--Employment Exchange

_____

_____

NOTE.

Women who are already engaged in any of the following occupations will not be accepted unless they bring with them a letter from their Employer or Head of Department stating that they have permission to volunteer:--

(i) Government Service.

(ii) Munition work.

(iii) Work in a Controlled Establishment.

(iv) Full-time work in an establishment engaged on contract   work for a Government Department.

(v) V.A.D. Military Hospitals and Red Cross Hospitals.

(vi) School Teaching.

(vii) Local Government Service.

No woman who is a National Service Volunteer or is employed in Agriculture will be accepted.

N.B.--Applicants are urged not to give up any present employment until they are called upon to do so.

(Part of the application form used in England by the Women's Land Army.)

WOMEN'S LAND ARMY

CONDITIONS AND TERMS.

There are three Sections of the Women's Land Army.

(1). AGRICULTURE.

(2). TIMBER CUTTING.

(3). FORAGE.

If you sign on for A YEAR and are prepared to go wherever you are sent, you can join which Section you like.

YOU PROMISE:--

1. To sign on in the Land Army for ONE YEAR.

2. To come to a Selection Board when summoned.

3. To be medically examined, free of cost.

4. To be prepared if PASSED by the Selection Board to take up work   after due notice.

5. TO BE WILLING TO GO TO WHATEVER PART OF THE COUNTRY YOU ARE SENT.

THE GOVERNMENT PROMISES:--

1. A MINIMUM WAGE to workers of 18/- a week. After they have passed   an efficiency test the wages given are £1 a week and upwards.

2. A short course of FREE INSTRUCTION if necessary.

3. FREE UNIFORM.

4. FREE MAINTENANCE in a Depôt for a term not exceeding 4 weeks if the worker is OUT OF EMPLOYMENT through no fault of her own.

5. FREE RAILWAY travelling, when taking up or changing Employment.

Image 1. *US Kanning Kitchen* [Photograph] At:
http://ohs.org/education/focus/home-front-world-war-
I.cfm

Printed in Great Britain
by Amazon